MEMOIRS OF A CRACKHEAD

This book is dedicated to anyone and everyone that I ever wronged while under the influence of crack.

And to my family who stuck by me no matter how bad it got. Thank you for never giving up on me.

Sincerely,

Russell Tolson, Jr.

MEMOIRS OF A CRACKHEAD

BASED ON A TRUE STORY

RICH D. FRASER
RUSSELL TOLSON JR.

Memoirs of a Crackhead by Rich D. Fraser and Russell Tolson

Published by Voxxity, LLC 5016 Rushlight Path Columbia, MD 21044

www.voxxity.com

Cover Design: Rich D. Fraser
Interior Design: Rich D. Fraser
Publisher: Voxxity, LLC
Editor: Azalaya Fraser, Eric Ingram

For permissions contact:
fraser@voxxity.com

ISBN-13: 978-1976454585

Printed by Create Space Resources

"Rehab did not get you on drugs and rehab won't get you off drugs either. Only you can do that."

-Russell Tolson Sr.

ACKNOWLEDGEMENTS

First and foremost, I'd like to thank Russell Tolson, Jr. for opening up his life and sharing with me his most personal moments in his battle with crack addiction. I know your bravery and willingness to share your whole truth – the good, the bad and the ugly – is undoubtedly what will reach the readers the most. I can say from my time working with you, that although you may have done A LOT of wrong in the past, today you are one of the most sincere, giving and honest people I've ever met. Thank you for trusting me to tell your story.

Next, I'd like to thank Kathy Tolson for helping us complete the book. Russell's crackhead memory wasn't always the most reliable, so having Kathy there to back him up and to elaborate on the entertaining details was a huge help!

I want to thank Marlon Green for the hours he spent transcribing the many audio interviews from which this book was written, and Eric Ingram for being a much needed third set of eyes and great editor.

Lastly, I couldn't have done this project without the help of my wonderful wife, Azalaya Fraser. I want to thank you for staying up with me night after night, going over the book chapter by chapter, and for being my "final polish" on everything I do. I know that with you by my side I can do anything – even write my first book! Your love and support of all my crazy ideas is truly what makes this all possible.

Sincerely,

Rich D. Fraser

TABLE OF CONTENTS

Minimum Crack Wage
Three-Way Calling

Ma, Loan Me Some Money
Public Assistance
The Prodigal Daughter
Last Man Standing
Dealing with Daddy
No Russell Allowed

Eviction Day
With Relatives Like Me, You Don't Need Enemies
Geekin'
The High Hero
Time's Up

Get It Together Russell
A New Beginning
To Love, Honor, and Respect
We're Movin' On Up
Standing Strong

Introduction

Question: What do you get when you take a neat freak with an Obsessive-Compulsive Disorder and introduce him to crack? The cleanest crack-head on the block! But enough bragging… After all, I didn't start out that way, of course. No, like just about everyone else, I mindlessly picked up the habits that turned me into the troubled junkie I was over time, and I can trace those habits back as far as my adolescence.

If I had to describe my childhood growing up in one word it would be "cramped." I lived in a three-bedroom house that was home to twelve people. That's right *twelve.* Not seven. Not nine. *Twelve.* Despite not being Asian, both my great-grandmother *and* grandmother lived with us. Despite not being Catholic, I had five sisters and two brothers. And despite being black, both my mother *and* father were hanging around, living under one roof, and taking up whatever remaining space an absentee parent might have provided upon their abandonment. My brother and I, who both slept on a pullout couch in the living room, had less privacy than two cellmates. And lying there at night I could only *dream* of my dad leaving my mom in stereotypical fashion and splitting up the family. Maybe then I'd *at least* have my own bed.

To make things more complicated, my father, who just *had* to stick around and take care of his responsibilities, was a stickler for cleanliness. We might have been poor, but we could've been on 'Lifestyles of the Broke But Spotless. I mean, if Mr. Clean would've come to our condemned home, he would've been like, "Daaammm, this place is clean! What'd y'all call me for?" For my father, it was all about pride and self-respect -- something that didn't have a dollar value attached to it, because if it did, we couldn't afford it. And of all the places to grow up learning the bourgeois belief "money can't buy you class," who would've thought it'd be in the hood. But that was my Dad for you. He was the only guy I knew that brought his work truck—a cement mixer—home and washed it. Yes, washed it! How many of you would do *that* today? The companies that *owned* the truck never even cared to wash those filthy rigs, but my father saw it as a reflection of him, and he wanted it to look good.

One day, his boss gave him the dirtiest, most filthy truck I'd ever seen. It looked like a dried turd barreling down the street at 50mph. He had the whole neighborhood running for their lives whilst holding their noses. Cans, dirt, dust, and trash everywhere. My father took it to the car wash, cleaned it inside and out, and took it back to the job. When his boss saw the truck, he couldn't believe it was the same one my father had taken only a few hours earlier. He looked it over in utter amazement and from that day on, gave my father the newest trucks in the fleet because he knew he would take care of them.

As amazing as it was that my father's self-respect and cleanliness led his bosses to respect him, his coworkers, on the other hand, couldn't have been *less* impressed. In fact, they were pissed. Now the boss expected them to keep *their* trucks clean too! My father would have made less enemies if he'd slept with everyone's wife, knocked up two, and illegally married one, than he did when he introduced a little turtle wax and water into the workplace.

Call it OCD, PCP, STD or my father's influence, but I, somehow, became just as anal about keeping my things clean. And that extended to my car, my clothes, my crib and my cojones. Yeah, I was that guy with the lifetime supply of pocket-sized bottles of hand sanitizer, SQUIRT-SQUIRT, suckers. I was obsessed. I hated junk, yet in an ironic twist of life, drug addiction transformed me into a junkie, a base head, dope fiend, pipe jockey, broken toilet seat salesman, a crackitute – aka a crackhead. *That's* when I became someone I barely recognized – someone whose actions were no longer driven by the self-respecting principles my father had instilled in me. I became someone I barely recognized and I did things I never imagined that I would do. And I was like that for decades, or a week. I don't remember.

But by the grace of God, everything is cool now and I have so many stories to tell you from my life as a sanitary crackhead. You'll either believe them or think they're too outlandish to be true. Some may make you laugh; others will upset you. There are even a few that will make you say WTF??! But good or bad, they're real, and they're my life. I survived these experiences only by the skin of my missing teeth. I've been beat up, shot at, evicted, homeless, and imprisoned, but thanks to Almighty God, I'm alive to implore you not to go down the same path as I did. The Bible says, "Life and death are in the power of the tongue and they that love it shall eat the fruit thereof." That ain't a lie. I could've said "no" to crack, but my curiosity got the best of me. And because of it, my life fell off-track for a moment. Now that I'm back on the good side, I want to reach out and help anybody and everybody who not only have drug problems, but are not living their greatest life. I'm talking to those in all walks of life who've made a bad decision and can't see a way out. I'm here to tell you there is a way out. All you have to do is take the first step and really ask yourself, "Are you going to choose life or death?" My two cents…Choose Life.

CHAPTER 1

Trouble Magnet

Most kids go to school to learn, not me. I was there to cut up and act a fool. "Having Fun" was my nickname and getting in trouble was my game. Everybody knew I was the kid that would do whatever you dared me to do. And don't double dare me or it was on and poppin'. I remember someone said, "I dare you to go in the girl's bathroom and write "Mrs. Johnson stinks on the wall." Ten seconds later I was in the girl's bathroom doing my first graffiti tag, "Miss Johnson stinks like poo." A couple of girls saw me and ran out screaming into the hall. My friends and I laughed so hard until my teacher, Mrs. Johnson, saw what I wrote on the bathroom wall. She glared at me and said, "Russell, did you write that?" "No," I said sheepishly. She already knew who did it. She yanked me by my arm and took me to the principal's office. As we passed my friends, they were still laughing, but I wasn't. Everyone would be outside playing at recess while I was stuck in the classroom writing "*I will not go in the girl's bathroom*" 500 times. I couldn't even count to 50 let alone 500, but there I was, imprisoned for recess. What makes it so bad is that I did another dare the very next day and ended up missing recess again. I was in detention so much, when my teacher asked the class, "Where's the one place you dream of going?" Some said, "France" or "Africa." I said, "Outside at recess." I was the only kid with a VIP pass to detention. I had my own seat and everything. I kept doing stupid stuff over and over again because doing what other kids were afraid to do was fun. It made me special, respected, and most importantly, cool.

Whenever I got in trouble, the principal would give me a lashing with a monstrous paddle from Medieval times. This was no ordinary paddle. The Devil made this one. It had holes in it so not only would it cut through the air with more speed, but when she hit you, the holes would suck your butt into the paddle like a Hoover vacuum. When she hit me, it sounded like somebody just got shot – POW! She would make me pull down my pants and underwear. Then I'd have to bend all the way over like a stripper and take a paddling from this frail woman. The first one stung to high-hell, but after that, the hits weakened. The whole time she was hitting me, I'd talk trash in my head, "Did you think those little butterfly swats are gonna stop me from being mischievous and getting into trouble? Hell no! The only thing it did was make me fearless.

My grandmother grew up with this crazy troublemaker named, Sam, so she began calling me Sam because I reminded her of him.

"Sam, whatchu done done now?" is how she greeted me every day when I got home from school.

"How you know I did something?"

"I know you. Look at you, you're guilty."

"I didn't do anything <u>today</u>," I'd say with a huge, Cheshire Cat grin plastered across my face. But she wasn't a fool. She knew her grandson was a magnet to trouble.

Silver Dollars

As a kid, it's hard being the broke one in your group of friends, especially when you all take a trip to the corner store. My friends were millionaires to me. They'd buy sodas <u>and</u> chips <u>and</u> candy <u>and</u> pickles. Meanwhile, my broke behind had to put penny candy on layaway. Then I'd have to stand there and watch them eat it all right in front of me. I tried to get them to share. I even gave them the poor Ethiopian boy starving face, complete with the signature fly in the eye, but they'd just laugh with their mouths full of yummy junk food. Standing on the sidelines and being left out is a terrible feeling when you're a kid… and an adult, too. I still feel that way today. Whether it's candy at the corner store, a burger at a fast food restaurant, or a ticket to the movies, a kid should have some money in his pocket in case he wants to buy something.

Every year, our church sponsored us to go to amusement parks, and my parents wouldn't give me a single dime for the trip. The first year I went was a nightmare. All of the kids were buying whatever they wanted at the park: popcorn, cotton candy, sodas, chocolate, but I was stuck with a soggy bologna and mayonnaise sandwich and hot bottled water that the church packed. I was determined not to go through that again, so when the next trip came around the following year, I found a way to get some money – big money!

My grandmother worked for the government and she collected freshly-printed silver dollars and two-dollar bills she received from her department. She kept the money in a can with a lock on it that would only open with a little key she kept on a chain somewhere in the room. I figured I'd borrow a dollar just to have some spending money and fit in with the other kids at the amusement park. Besides, she wouldn't miss a dollar, right?

I tried to open the can with a paperclip, a bobby pin, a toothpick, but nothing worked. So I began watching her like a hawk to see where she kept the key. Finally, I discovered she kept the key in her sewing kit in her drawer. I took a silver dollar to the amusement park and bought so much stuff that the kids thought I was rich. I bought whatever I wanted, and I loved the freedom I had. I also loved the attention.

From that point on, I'd take a couple silver dollars whenever I needed some spending money. I didn't think I'd ever get caught because I wasn't taking a lot of money at once. I figured I'd stop and she'd never find out what I did. But greedy me, I kept going back to get more and more. It got to the point where I was withdrawing money faster than she was depositing it, but I never felt an ounce of guilt over it. I fell in love with the feeling of stealing. It was my first high.

Karma

Years down the line, I went to 7-11 to buy a waffle cone on a hot night in the city. I took it to the cashier, paid for it, got my change, but forgot to get a receipt as I normally would. I headed for the door as I started chowing down on it.

Suddenly the Indian cashier barked, "Hey, you didn't pay!"

"Yes, I did. I just gave you the money."

"You didn't give me money!"

I walked out the door and took another bite of the ice cream. I knew I paid for it. Next thing I know, this sucker-punk grabbed me from behind, put me in some Ju-Jitsu head lock, dragged me back into the store and made me call my father. My father came up there with that look in his eye like I committed murder or something.

"What happened?" he asked.

The cashier told him his side. As soon as he finished, I jumped in to tell my side.

"Daddy, I didn't steal no ice cream. I paid him. He's lying! Look!" I pulled out more than enough money than the ice cream was worth. "I paid for the ice cream."

"Since you have so much money, you should have paid him."

"But I did."

"Shut up! This man has no reason to lie on you."

I couldn't believe it! My father took the cashier's side and didn't believe a word I said. I was totally innocent this time! Figures, all the time I was doing crazy things, I never got caught for them. Now, the one time I didn't do anything, I get blamed for doing something.

When we got home, my father followed me up the creaking stairs to my room and proceeded to lay a butt whooping on me like you wouldn't believe. I knew it was going to be a bad whippin' because he started stretching before he whipped me. When he was all limber, he looked into my crying eyes.

"You're the one that's been stealing all this time."

"I didn't steal that ice cream."

"I'm not talking about ice cream! I'm talking about the silver dollars out of your grandmother's can."

"See, what had happened was…"

It turns out that all this time my grandmother knew someone was taking her money. She told my father, but she never said anything to us kids. They just sat back and waited to see who was doing it, and it all fell down on me. Damn you, Karma. Damn you.

CHAPTER 2

First Job, First Smoke

When I was twelve years old, I started working for a nice old man named Mr. Dickey, a janitor at an elementary school in the neighborhood. There were a few of us kids working for him. He'd give us $1.50 a day to empty the trashcans, mop and sweep the floors, and clean up litter outside. It helped me stay out of trouble and earn some honest money. We had no real interests then, so all we did was take the money right to the store and spend every cent of it on candy.

It was around this time that I met Garland "D-Guy". He was the coolest boy around because he dressed sharper than a Ginsu knife. He always came out dressed to the nines. He had a job, so he could afford to look good. He'd have on a dress shirt, slacks, and nice shoes. He saw how hard I worked for Mr. Dickey and one day pulled me aside and said, "Hey, Russ, when you're ready to make some real money, come holla at me." I saw his spiffy car and his sharp clothes and I chimed back, "When can I start?" He immediately took me under his wing and let me hang with him because he knew I was cool. He would take me shopping downtown and buy me a pair of pants and a shirt. He'd buy me stuff that my parents couldn't even dream of buying me. That's what made him the man to me. He was the king and acted like it.

That summer, I ended up getting a real job pumping gas at a gas station on the weekends. They knew I was a hard worker that didn't slack up. And I was their best worker, too. This was back in the days when you got full service at the gas station. I would clean a customer's windows, check their oil and tire pressure, and get them something to drink all before the gas was finished pumping. Eventually, they showed me how to read the pumps at the end of the night. Big mistake. I learned that the pumps controlled the money and whoever controlled the pumps could make extra cash by manipulating the readings. Man, I began manually rolling back the numbers on the pumps, creating the misconception that less money was made. Then I wrote down the rollback number in the books and submitted the amount of money that matched that number. Every night I ended up walking away with a couple hundred dollars in my pocket. I was suddenly making big money, and instead of buying candy like before, I began dressing, spending my bread on better clothes, hoping to look like D-Guy.

I'll never forget the day D-Guy was smoking a cigar in front of me.

I said, "Let me try that."

"Go ahead."

He handed it to me like it wasn't a big deal. I put that cigar to my mouth, inhaled, and my whole face turned beet red. My throat and lungs were on fire. I began choking.

"Chew on this," he said, handing me a pack of bubble gum.

I shoved four pieces in my mouth, and by golly, it worked. I stopped choking.

"You never smoked before have you?"

"No," I said as I got myself together.

"I'll never let you smoke a cigar with me again. You had me scared for a minute. I thought you were going to die."

My chest was still burning. "I thought I was going to die, too." It was clear then, that smoking would not be my favorite choice of drug.

Hooking School

But by the time high school came around, alcohol certainly was. That September, I think I was a freshman in high school. Out of the kindness of my heart, I decided to give my new unsuspecting teachers a break from my legendary elementary school antics by hooking classes every day. I'd catch the bus to school with no plans of going to class. As soon as the bus dropped us off at school, I'd leave the premises and hook up with my boys. The first thing we did was pull out a bottle of liquor and drink till we got drunk. When we ran out, whoever had money would buy the next round. That's all we did all day: drink, talk trash, jone on each other, and laugh.

Tony would say, "Did y'all see Mike's mother last night?"

"No," Jimmy answered.

"I know you didn't," Tony would smile, "because she was in my bed."

"I know you ain't talking about my mother!" Mike would say. "Your mother looks like Leon Spinks and King Kong had a baby!"

We'd laugh and drink as they talked about each other's mommas. The more we drank, the wilder the jokes got. "Your momma so fat, she sat on a quarter and a booger shot out of George Washington's nose." We'd damn near piss on ourselves from laughing so hard.

One time, we got so drunk, we barely made it back to school to catch the bus to get home. Walking the three miles home wasn't fun at all, so somebody had to keep us updated on the time. On the occasions when we got back to school early, we'd go to the library and pass out until the bell rang to get on the bus. We were a bunch of drunks at 13 & 14-years old. We needed to go to AA, seriously. *Hello, my name is Russell, and I'm a teenage alcoholic. Hello, Russell.*

My parents had no idea I hooked school so much, and they surely didn't know I drank alcohol. My father would have torn me up with that belt if he knew.

The only way I kept up in my studies was because I had a classmate that covered for me. I don't know if she liked me, felt sorry for me, or if she was just cool like that, but she always had my back. On the days that I didn't play hooky, I would sleep through whatever class I was in. My classmate would tap me on my shoulder.

"Russell, wake up."

"What?" I'd say groggily.

"It's time to go. You missed everything the teacher went over, but here are the notes. I wrote them down for you."

"Thank you."

I wasn't stupid – I took advantage of those notes and studied them. I passed thanks to her.

Sophomore Blues

I got really bad in high school. I grew tired of hanging around D-Guy all his small time hustles and instead started hanging with older guys… *that were into stealing even bigger things*. These guys were stealing cars, breaking into houses, and taking whatever they saw that wasn't nailed down. I hung around them for the excitement, and I learned a lot in the process.

My buddy, Earnest, whom I would ride bikes with to Anacostia Park, was hanging with me every step of the way. We left school almost every day and went to the burger joint at the bottom of the hill. It was our official hanging spot. We'd get burgers, fries, and sodas padding our stomachs before consuming the drug of the day. Earnest would always go get some wine, cigarettes, and weed, and after eating, we'd step outside and partake. I tried weed, but I didn't like it. All it did was make me get sleepy and then want to eat up everything in the house. That wasn't for me. I enjoyed drinking. Give me some wine or some liquor and I'm good. Another thing that wasn't for me, heroin. I tried everything else, but not dope. One time in the locker room, a buddy of mine, Frank, was about to shoot up, but he didn't want to do it by himself. He looked at me.

"You want to try it?"

"No, man. I don't do that."

"Stop acting scared."

"I ain't scared. Heroin ain't my get down."

He smirked like he was up to something. "I'm going to get you high on this dope."

"No, you ain't."

He came toward me, and I took off like a cat at a dog show. He chased me around the entire gym with the needle. After not catching me for about a minute, he went back into the locker room and got high. From that day on, I was petrified of needles.

I went to class so rarely that I sometimes forgot my schedule. I mean, I was ripping and running around town so much during school hours for all of my high school years that I knew I wasn't going to graduate. I was prepared to face the embarrassment of watching all my friends move on while I was left back for another year.

But when they put out the list of names of the people graduating, guess what – I was somehow on it! I graduated. I couldn't believe it that I passed! 'Till this day, I still don't know how I graduated. I never went to class. My family was so proud of me because they knew without a doubt I wasn't going to graduate. My sister said straight-up, "This dumb boy ain't coming out of school because he never went in the school." They all had jokes, but the jokes stopped at my graduation. When they gave me that diploma and let me walk across that stage, nobody could tell me nothing. Man, I thought I was King Kong!

CHAPTER 3

Get The Pledge, It's About To Get Dusty!

After Earnest and I graduated, we still kept hanging together. We hit it off so well for so long that we began calling each other brothers. I had his back and he had mine – and we needed each other while entering the game we were about to get into.

The city was going crazy over a new drug known as "angel dust" and "love boat." They called it "love boat" because when you smoked it, you felt like you were in love because the high was so intense. It was made by sprinkling PCP, a drug originally introduced as an anesthetic, on weed. People were going crazy for this stuff. And since I was always looking for a way to make money, I wanted in.

Earnest knew a guy that made the PCP liquid, which we called "water." We got lucky because we were introduced to a chemist that made PCP. It was hard as hell to find one, which is why demand was so high, and here he was right here in our presence. All I saw were dollar signs. Buying weed was a major overhead expense. We didn't have money and time to buy weed, put the PCP liquid on it, then measure the weed and put it into bags or foil. That process was small thinking and I didn't want to nickel and dime my way to getting paid. I wanted the big dollars. So Earnest and I bought tiny bottles in bulk from the store, put the "water" in them, and hit the streets selling the main ingredient for people to get high. We figured they could make their own 'dust' when they wanted, get high as often as they wanted, and make it as strong they wanted it.

See, the beauty of 'dust' is you could put the 'water' on things other than weed. If you didn't want to chase down the weed man, or if you didn't want to spend money, you could get the same high for much cheaper by putting the 'water' on tobacco or parsley flakes – you could even put it on Fruit Loops! I don't care what you put our 'water' on, you were going to get high. It was so strong; just one whiff and you'd get a super high from it.

We charged $400 per bottle, and just as Earnest and I thought, we sold out in a few hours. People couldn't get enough of what we were selling. We'd bottle more 'water,' and they'd buy it just as fast as before. They loved what we were selling because they knew it was potent. After a few puffs, you were guaranteed to be hallucinating and zoning into another world… into another galaxy! That dust was so good, I had to try it. That was a major mistake.

I broke the #1 rule of drug dealing – Never get high on your own supply. But there I was enjoying it just as much as my clients were. I'd buy parsley flakes, put them in a Ziploc bag, put a little 'water' in there, shake it up really good, let it set for 10-15 minutes, roll up a joint, and then smoke it. Man, I'd get so high, I'd forget I didn't like smoking. On this stuff, you forget to breathe; you'd forget where you put your bike, your car, or whatever. You'd be so high, you'd have to chill until the high wore off. You couldn't function until then. See, when you get high, the whole world gets closer and closer, and the next thing you know you'd black out and you're in another world, a dream world, and that's what I liked. I'd be high and ghetto-fabulous. I'd know all of these people; they all wanted to be around me. I'd sit there and say to myself, "Wow, I'm going to get rich." I'd be getting rich and making money on top of money. Suddenly, as soon as the high was over, I'd wake up and say, "What the hell? What happened? I was getting paid, but now I'm broke again." I'd have to roll another joint to hurry up and get back to that dream before it disappeared forever. But I'd never get back to the same dream. And that was a nightmare.

Another time, while I was getting high, I got on a jet without a pilot and I was cool with that. I didn't think about the imminent crash in my future because I was enjoying the ride – I was enjoying the high. All aboard 'The Love Boat.' Fasten your seatbelts and leave your pipes in the upright position…

Wheeling and Drug Dealing

I always wanted to be big and famous. I liked to stand out from everyone else, and that's easy to do if you have some money and some nerve. There's nothing fun about being part of the crowd, but that's exactly what I was in my new job as an electrician.

To cope, I used to get my hair processed every Friday. My sisters were so mad at me because my hair was so much better than theirs. I'd press it back, curl it, then take the comb and comb it into a curl look. Then I'd throw on my fur coat, slip on my fur hat, grab my handbag and be out the door. Man, you couldn't tell me nothing. People that saw me didn't know if I was a pimp or a hustler, but, either way, they considered me a star.

I liked dressing sharp, riding in nice cars, and getting high, and so did Earnest. So, what did we do? We combined all of those things. We began renting limousines in our fancy clothes – we had nowhere special to go – we just wanted to ride in style. We'd tell the driver to drive us around the city, and we sat in the back drinking, snorting coke, and smoking dust. We'd roll through uptown, downtown, Georgetown, whatever town, and had a party the whole way.

We'd stop at a busy club just to see what was going on. When we pulled up, they thought stars were coming up in there. They thought we were somebody important, but we were nobodies. We'd walk in with our suits sharp, hats cocked, handbags, and our canes – acting like we owned the place. The cane was actually a cocaine cane, but it appeared to simply be a walking cane with a ball at the top. If you held the middle of the cane in your left hand and pulled on the top of the cane with your right, you'd have a sword. If you unscrewed the ball, it had a secret area inside where I kept cocaine. I always carried coke, but no one knew where it was because I was smart.

Anyway, ladies couldn't take their eyes off of us. We drew all the attention from the moment we stepped foot in the joint. We'd stay a little while and then drive to another club and do the same thing. Some nights, we'd stop at four or five clubs, and in each one we'd buy drinks like it wasn't a thang. I was working as an electrician by day and Earnest and I were selling bottles of 'water' day and night, so we had plenty of money to throw around. I use to bring a girl home every single night from the club. Some women were curious, some wanted to get spoiled by some players, and others wanted to be in our limelight. We never went after them, they'd come over to us on their own.

"Hi."

"How are you doing?"

"You look very nice. I like your suit."

"Thank you, baby. What can I do for you?"

"I just wanted to meet you. What do you do?"

"I'm a businessman."

"Are you a pimp or a gangster?"

I'd laugh off those questions, but I'd keep them curious. The next thing you knew, Earnest and I would pick who we wanted, take them out of the club, and then we'd party in private all night long. If they wanted to play, we had whatever type of game they wanted. Me and Earnest were the Abbott & Costello of water sales. We were a phenomenal two-man team. We worked off each other and had codes for things. Like if he wanted one of the girls we brought back to the apartment, he would 'accidentally' spill a little of his drink on her so he could cop a quick feel. If I wanted a certain girl, I would make up a song about her specific features to cue Earnest on who I wanted. "I can't wait to kiss the girl with the cantaloupes in her blouse." A few nights, we both wanted to serve the same girl. Let's just say, some nights, one girl got a drink and a song about them. The next morning I'd put on my electrician uniform and go back to work.

People loved getting high; they loved that 'love boat;' and they loved the quality of the 'water' I was selling. I couldn't get a break because people were always calling me wanting more of it. The demand for the 'water' was so great, people stopped paying their actual water bill at home to buy my 'water.' There was so much money, I was practically tripping over cash in my house. I had a couch made out of cash. I ate cash flakes. It was ridiculous.

What's a young guy supposed to do with all that money? Fancy clothes and going to the clubs in limousines was cool, but I finally decided I needed my own car. And I wanted the flyest car out there. I wanted it to be fancy. I wanted it to stop traffic every time I rode by.

I put up the money and I had a friend help me with the paperwork. And Walla, I was soon rolling in my first car – a 1977 Buick Regal. That baby was slick, too! It was red with a white rag top and velvet seats that were so soft that you felt like you were sitting on a red velvet cake couch. The chemist I was getting 'water' from had a connection with a guy that puts remote control on cars. He wired my car so that when I played music, neon lights would blink under the dashboard to the beat. This was some real gangster stuff! It really set the mood especially when I had a woman in the car and we were getting high. People started tripping off fancy spinning rims in the 90s, but I had them back in the 70s when nobody else did. I rolled up and down the streets looking like a million dollars. I was so flashy that people thought Rick James or somebody was driving by. Earnest had a red Ford Marquis that was slick, but it wasn't as slick as my car.

As I was driving my new car off the lot, I got paged by this biker dude that rolled around on a huge Harley Davidson. I found a pay phone and called him back.

"What's up? I just got a page from this number."

"This is Bernard. Man, this stuff you sold me ain't nothing."

"What do you mean?" I was confused.

"You know what I mean. You sold me a bad batch."

This cat obviously had the wrong guy. "You sure you bought it from me?"

"Yeah, I'm sure I bought it from you. I paged you, didn't I? This is Russell, ain't it?"

"I'll be right there."

I get to his apartment building; get off the elevator, and the first thing I smell are the chemicals in the hallway. I said to myself, *this fool is going to get me and him locked up!* I knocked on his door, and he opened it.

"Do you have a good batch for me?"

"Just let me in. We'll talk about it inside."

I walk in his house and followed the smell to the kitchen. This fool left the bag of dust open in the refrigerator and it had everything smelling like dust. I sealed the bag and closed the refrigerator. I picked up his bottle of 'water' off the counter and smelled it. It was perfect. I screwed the top on, placed it in the refrigerator, and turned around only to find him staring at me.

"Where's the good water?" he asked.

"Man, your water is good."

"No, it's not."

I saw that his eyes were red, so I knew he was high. He just didn't know he was high. I said, "Okay, tell me what you did."

"I did what you told me to do. I put the weed in that bag you just had, I put a few drops of water in it, let it set for about twenty minutes, and then I smoked it, but nothing happened.

Now if you're not going to give me a new bottle, then give me my money back."

This joker was crazy to think I was giving him $400 back just because he didn't know he was high. I cracked the windows so the place could air out from the smell of the chemicals.

"What are you doing?"

"I'm opening the windows so that people won't call the police. I smelled the chemicals when I got off the elevator."

"Shhhhh," he said as he stared out of the window. "Be quiet… Do you hear that?"

I didn't hear a damn thing. "Hear what?"

"The moon. It's right there. It's whispering to me."

I just shook my head and frowned at him. "What do you see other than the moon?"

"I don't see nothing because it's dark outside."

I heard enough. "Man, you are high out of your mind. Look at your watch."

He looked down at it.

"It's one o'clock in the afternoon. That's not the moon, that's the sun, and it's bright as hell outside."

Then he looked at me like I was crazy. "That's the moon. I'm not stupid. Ask them what time of the day it is."

I was confused. "Ask who?"

"The friends you brought with you. Them over there."

I looked next to me where he was pointing like a damn fool, then I came to my senses. "Man, ain't nobody here but me and you!"

"No, you brought Thelma from '*Good Times*' with you."

"If I was with Thelma from '*Good Times*,' do you think I'd be here with you?"

"Ask her if I can get her autograph."

This joker was super high. "Man, you done lost your mind. This is what you need to do…"

I told him to keep the bag closed, keep the bottle in the refrigerator, and not to go anywhere until he could tell the difference between the sun and the moon. As I left his apartment, someone asked me if I knew where they could get some love boat.

"You have $400."

CHAPTER 4

Crime Pays

There's a cap on the amount of money you can make when you're an employee. I was making solid money as an electrician, and tons of money selling 'water.' I was a fat cat that wanted to eat more and more. If an opportunity came that could make me more money, I jumped on it with the quickness.

In addition to hanging with Earnest, I started hanging out more with a group of guys that I smoked dust with. These guys were crime heavyweights. They played for big stakes. Big stakes, big money. And I like big money. The ringleader would find a job to do, which we called finding a lick or a caper. He'd go over the plan, we'd steal stuff, and then we'd split up the money. The ringleader was smart. He'd set everything up and was the first to get paid, but he'd never go with us. If something went down, he was never on the scene to get arrested. He did the planning in advance, but it was always his brother, me, and a few other guys doing the actual crime.

On this particular day, the ringleader gave me an old, raggedy, stolen car and told me to pick up the rest of the guys. When I pulled up, the guys came out with guns and pillow cases and got in the car. I said, "What's going on?"

"We're robbing a bank."

I'm not a punk, and I was living very reckless, so I said, "What do you want me to do?"

"Take this gun and do what we tell you to do when we get there."

I went along because I knew we were going to get paid and we weren't going to kill anybody. We were just going to get some free money. Banks had all the money, and all I was thinking about was how much money I was going to make. I didn't consider the trouble I could get into.

We drove to southern Maryland to rob a bank in Charles County. While driving there, we went over the plan again and again. We were going to put on masks. One person was going to guard the door, one was going to disarm the guard, one would hold the customers at gunpoint, and the other was going to collect the money from the tellers. We were then going to get back in the car, drive to a second location, ditch the getaway car for another car, and then go back to PG County and split the money. Very simple, right?

Everything went as planned until we exited the bank. As we dashed for the car, there was this guy staring at me like we slept together last night. Out of all of us, he zeroed in on me, so I pulled my mask off like an idiot to look at him to see what he was looking at. He wasn't scared or anything, but he kept looking. The dudes were like, "Let's go!" I headed to the car and hopped in, all the while staring at this guy like, "What's your damn problem?" We sped off, but that guy stayed on my mind.

The Charles County Sheriff's Department was like roaches. As we drove to our destination, they popped out from everywhere. It seems like they were coming out the ground. Before we could get to our second car, the police were already in that area.

"What's the backup plan?" David asked.

"I don't know," I said, "but we have to get out of this car because they're looking for it!"

Tyrone said, "Let's park and wait in the woods over there until they leave the area."

That was the only thing that made sense at that moment, so we sat in the woods and waited. I can't believe we were sitting there with the bags of money and the guns – all the evidence was on us! We all were paranoid as hell. Our adrenaline was pumping hard. Suddenly, we heard movement coming over the hill.

"Sic 'em!" said a commanding voice.

It was a policeman letting go of his K-9. When I heard him say, "sic 'em," I was gone! The dog came after us full speed. I flew through them woods like an Olympic gold medalist! I never ran so fast before in my life. With a bag of money in my hand, I outran my fellow crime partners, the dog and anything else that was behind me.

I came to a lake that stood between the K-9 and freedom. I watched a lot of TV and they always said if you're going to run away from the police, water will throw off a dogs scent, and so would the smell of pepper. I didn't have any pepper so I dashed through the water without a second thought.

Nighttime came and I was still walking back home to PG County, but now I was on the main road. When I saw a car coming, I'd scurried off the road until they passed, then I'd get back on the road. I got all the way to PG County. I was tired of walking. My knees and back were killing me. I came upon a guy in his yard smoking a cigarette. I approached him.

"Man, look, I need a ride home, and it's not far from here. If you take me, I'll give you $100."

"Where do you live?"

"Seat Pleasant."

He reached into his pocket and pulled out his keys. "Let's go."

I reached in my bag of money, pulled out $100, and he took me home. I had him drop me off a nice distance from my house because I didn't want him to know where I lived. I thought to myself, *Police dogs can trace my shoes,* so I took them off and threw them in the bushes. I walked the rest of the way to my partner's house. We got there and put all the money out and realized we hit the jackpot — $30,000. That was a whole lot of money back then. We split the money up six ways, but one guy was missing. We later found out he got caught and he snitched on everybody. I got lucky because they didn't have enough information on me to know who I was. And since he snitched, his part of the money got divided between the five of us. Just think, him running his mouth gave me a bigger payday. Running from a police dog, trashing a set of clothes and a pair of shoes, and spending $100 on a ride ended up earning me $5,900. That's not bad for a day's work.

A fancy car wasn't the goal, it was just a step along the way. The ultimate goal was to get a house. Now that I had that lump sum of money from the bank job, I looked around for a nice house. I found a beautiful townhouse in Kettering,

Maryland. I put a down payment on it with some of the bank money and I got the keys. At the time, Sugar Ray Leonard was the WBA Welterweight Champion of the World in boxing and he lived in my neighborhood. He had millions of dollars and a real career, and there I was living down the street from him with stolen money. That goes to show you that money can get you into places you really don't belong.

I wasn't riding around the city with Earnest as much as I was before because I got another job. In addition to being an electrician, selling 'water' to make dust, and stealing with the heist crew, I got a job working the door of a club. That gave me access to more people because everybody had to go through me to get inside. More access meant more networking, more networking meant more money.

I met lots of interesting people on the job including the daughter of a famous singer. Her name was Bunny and she was dating a football player that I went to high school with. She'd come to the club all the time. I used to look out for her just because I was cool with her boyfriend. We eventually became really good friends, but I didn't know who she was related to. One day, an entourage surrounded a man as they came to the door. The women were smiling at the man, hugging on him, and just all up in his face. I let them all in, but I was curious to know who they were.

Bunny was next to me. "Who is that man over there?" I asked her.

"You don't know who that is? He's my dad."

"Well, who is he?"

She told me the music group her father was in.

"Get out of here! That's your father?"

Knowing her had its perks, but I never took advantage of them despite how good they looked at the time.

The owner of the club actually owned another club across town, so I didn't always have a set of eyes looking over my shoulder. I was slick on the job. If there was one person trying to get in, I'd hook him or her up and let them in for free. If five girls came up, I'd give the club half and keep half. The club was always packed, and the money I turned in from admission was a lot of money, so the guy never knew what was going on. He was making lots of money from the door and even more from the bar.

Him not being around not only meant I had access to more money – it also gave me access to his girlfriend. I didn't mean to get close with her, but she was the bartender, and it's hard not to get better acquainted with them because you see them all the time and they make your drinks. We were really cool, and she was fine, too. But I wasn't pushing up on her like all the men that came there, and I think she found that attractive. Eventually, we started hanging out together after work. We'd leave the club early in the morning and go get something to eat. We talked so much and told so many war stories that before we knew it, the sun was coming up. The next thing you know, we started getting our food to go and going back to my place. Instead of the sun rising while we were in the restaurant, it was rising while she was lying in my bed.

We were dating and having a good time, until the owner found out about us. Everything was cool on my end. I knew she was still with him, so I kept things discreet. She did her thing, and I did mine. We had a nice thing going, but when he found out, that joker fired me on the spot. That was a fun job, too. Man.

Who Robbed A Bank?!

My uncle was a DC police officer in the fugitive department. He wasn't a fool; he knew I was running the streets at night when I got off work.

"What have you been up to, Russell?"

"I ain't been up to nothing," I'd routinely tell him.

"You've been doing something because I heard your name out there."

"Out where?"

"Out in the streets and on my scanner."

"You ain't hear my name. I'm not the only Russell out there."

"Uh-huh. They're watching you."

"They're wasting their time watching me. I'm just an honest electrician."

We went back and forth like that for years, and I always brushed him off. I didn't care what he was talking about because it didn't apply to me. I thought he was trying to scare me into giving him information or maybe he wanted me to fear him. I don't know. Then came the day he called me with a different approach.

"What's up, Russell?"

"Nothing?"

"You know they have a warrant out for you?"

"For who?"

"For you."

"For what?"

"For bank robbery?" he said, then he got quiet.

I knew he was listening to my voice for a clue of my innocence or guilt. "It wasn't me."

He saw right through my façade. "Look, here's your choice, you can turn yourself in or I can come get you."

"You're going to come and get me?" I laughed at him.

"I'm serious. Let me and your dad bring you in. That will look better for you."

I was a little shaken up, but I still didn't believe him. "What exactly did you hear that had my name in it?"

"Some guy named Kenny set up a bank robbery in southern Maryland. They caught one of the robbers, and he gave us Kenny's name. After being locked up for a few months, Kenny accepted a plea deal that was contingent of giving up the one robber they didn't have the name of – the name Russell."

Damn! I thought I had gotten away with my part of the bank robbery. I thought about what my uncle said and decided to turn myself in. I got a ride to the police station and approached the officer at the front desk.

"I'm here to turn myself in on a warrant."

"What's your name?"

"Russell."

He went through the system very slowly. "We don't have a warrant for you."

I was so relieved. It was as if 1,000 pounds was lifted off of my shoulders. I was already planning how high I was going to get to celebrate. But as I went to the door as a free man, the cop yelled,

"Hold it!"

"Huh?" I asked as I looked over my shoulder and held the door open.

"Let me check in one more place." He fumbled around for two minutes. "Oh yeah, you're a bank robber. We do have a warrant for you. Come on back."

My heart dropped. I was like, *oh, no! My uncle was right. I'm going to jail!*

He cuffed me up on the spot, and a white officer took me away.

He said, "You have two things against you: You're Black and you don't live down here."

"What do you mean?"

He stopped and looked at me. "You don't live in this neighborhood and you're Black," he said in a slow, stern voice.

"Oh my god. I'm down here in redneck country? They're going to kill me up in here!"

I went to court with good representation. I paid the lawyer $10,000 cash to get me off this charge — and ironically I paid him with half the money I stole from the bank.

He was very optimistic. "You probably won't do more than 17 months on probation because you don't have a record and you've never been locked up before."

"I'm fine with that. I can do 17 months."

My whole family came to court to support me. The judge started reading off charges.

"We're going to give you five years, consecutive to five years…consecutive to five years…"

I didn't understand what he was rambling about. I looked to my lawyer and said, "What in the world does consecutive mean?"

"You have to do X amount of years for one crime. After you do that time, you'll begin doing the next set of years for the next crime."

The judge kept rambling on, "…Armed Robbery, Attempted Murder, False imprisonment, Handgun Violation, Kidnapping, Resisting Arrest…"

The tension and anxiety bubbled within me. Finally he raised his gavel.

"The court is advised to sentence the defendant to 200 years!" and he slammed the gavel.

I almost pissed on myself. "Oh, man! I can't do all that time!"

"Calm down," my lawyer said.

His words went in one ear and out the other. "Ain't nobody living to be 200-years old! My heart can't take this!" I proclaimed as I grabbed my chest like Fred Sanford. *I'm ready to die, Elizabeth! Right now!*

Steel Bars On the Horizon

The six months I had until sentencing gave me time to get my head together. I accepted the fact that I was heading to jail, so I began putting my affairs in order. I had to dissolve my partnership with Earnest. That hurt me because it was a major money maker. Now the entire operation was his, and that included all of my customers. I also had to figure out what to do with my car. Lastly, I had to set up an arrangement with my new townhouse. I ended up giving a woman access to my money and she had to make the monthly payments on the house for me. I don't know why because I wasn't getting out for 200 years. I told Bunny, the daughter of the singer, what was going on, and she had a different perspective on everything.

"Are you serious?" she asked in shock.

"I'm serious, baby."

"200 years! That doesn't make sense."

"That's exactly what I said! How are they going to give me more time than I can live?"

She shook her head. "You do have another option. I'm moving to Atlanta."

"What's the option you're thinking about?"

"I'm moving to Atlanta. What you ought to do is come with me down there."

"Just leave and never come back?"

"Yes. Don't worry about going to court. All you have to do is get on the plane with me and you'll remain free."

"And just break the law?"

"It's not like you haven't broken the law before. That's how you got your ass in this position."

I laughed so hard at what she said. Not much was funny during that time, but she got me to loosen up and make me feel a little better.

"I'll think about that, baby."

"You do that. Keep in mind that you have nothing to lose. I mean, 200 years means you'll be in jail forever. Just come to Atlanta with me and don't worry about anything. You can stay with me free of charge until you get on your feet."

"Thank you, Bunny. That means a lot to me.

She was really looking out for me, and I appreciated that. I went straight to the library and began researching law. It felt funny being awake in a library. I was only used to sleeping in them. I looked up the law and found out that Maryland didn't have a statute of limitations. That means if I went down to Georgia and stayed, and something happened and I had to go back home to Maryland, I would still have to do the original 200 years plus extra time for evading court. It was a hard decision, but I figured I'd take my chances and go to jail. Bunny's offer was tempting, but I chose jail over Atlanta.

I went back to court like a lamb being walked into the lions' den. My lawyer got the 200-year sentence knocked down to 17 years, but I still wasn't happy. I was mad at my lawyer when I should have been fortunate he got 183 years off my sentence.

"I have to do 17 years for my first offense? I haven't done nothing! I ain't rob no bank."

I was going to shout from the mountaintop that I was innocent, but I was guilty as hell. The guy that saw my face when I took off my mask during the robbery testified against me in court and the guy that got caught testified against me. That was more than enough to send me down the river. Taking that mask off my head when I walked out of the bank was going to cost me 17 years of my life!

CHAPTER 5

30 Days in the County

My lawyer brought me great news. He was able to get The State to offer me a special deal which guaranteed a particular date for my release if I signed a simple contract. It stated that I would be in minimum security if I kept up my end of the deal and all I had to do was keep my nose clean. I couldn't believe it, but there it was in writing! I was going to do less than the 17 years I'd been given and there was no way I was going to pass that up. I don't care if it was 16 years, that's still 365 days less than 17. It turns out I'd actually only have to do approximately five years if I and stayed out of trouble, and that's just what I was going to do…at least I hoped so.

I thought they were going to send me straight to the penitentiary, but instead they sent me to the county jail. So there I was locked up. I had to do 30 days there to acclimate me, I guess. Whatever the case, the first night was the scariest thing I'd seen in my life. It was dark, cold. The bed was hard as coal, and there were strange sounds that seemed to be coming from every direction in the thick blackness. It was so scary that if they opened my gate, I would have tried to close it with the quickness. I was alone with my thoughts – and my thoughts were kicking my behind. I regretted going on that bank robbery job over and over again that night. Part of me said I should have jumped out of that car and went about my business when they got in the car with guns and pillowcases. The other part of me was happy I saved the money from the bank robbery because I was able to pay the lawyer with the bank's money. If it weren't for me saving the bank money, I would be doing 200 years.

When morning came, I was tired because I didn't sleep well. Then they brought me a TV dinner to eat and the anxiety of being locked up smacked me in the face again. I wanted to eat a nice steak, drink some Hennessy, or maybe have a burger and fries with a cold soda, but being in jail canceled all of that. All the money I had at home couldn't help me one bit.

They eventually let me out of my cell.

"What's going on?" I asked the guard.

"You can have some free time to take a shower or have recreation time. It's your choice."

I wasn't a damn kid, so I didn't need recreation time like a kid going to recess, but I wasn't stupid enough to go take a shower because I'd have to get naked in front of other men. I didn't know anyone there, so I sure wasn't trusting the shower area. I figured I'd be a little kid and go to recess.

I walked around a little bit and also talked to a couple of guys. An hour later, I was back in my cell for the rest of the day. I couldn't believe it! They only let you out for an hour per day! What about the other 23 hours? I sat in the cell feeling dumber than the night before, but I knew I couldn't let depression sink in. Instead of thinking about the choices that resulted in me getting locked up, I chose to think about all of the fun Earnest and I had when we were getting high, going to clubs, and getting all the women. Being in there wouldn't be so bad if I had a drink or two, but all I had was water. And not that kind of 'water.'

This Is Real Jail!

My 30 days were up. As I was on the bus heading to the penitentiary, I was really enjoying the rustic scenery from the bus window. I hadn't seen anything but steel bars and a gray and dingy cell for a month straight. But as we began approaching a massive cement castle with 20-foot-high steel walls around the perimeter, the beauty of the outside quickly faded away.

The correctional officers hustled us off the bus and escorted us inside. And man, beyond the walls was something straight out of a horror movie. As we entered 'the cage,' the inmates were bouncing around looking like wild animals. They were yelling, screaming, and banging on things. I thought to myself, "Maybe they're on the 'love boat?'"

"You're going to be my girl!" one muscular inmate yelled at the guy in front of me.

"You're going to be my bitch!" another wild-eyed guy yelled at the guy in back of me.

Then one looked at me. I turned my head as fast as humanly possible. *Where in the world am I?! Lord, get me out of here! I can't take this!*

The guards led all of us new inmates to a room and the door slammed shut behind us. Finally! I was glad to be away from all that noise.

"Alright, boys, take off your clothes, put them in your trash bag, and put on your uniforms."

The uniform consisted of a jumpsuit, black boots, and a pair of socks.

"Okay, boys, step over here and get your property."

The property consisted of a toothbrush, toothpaste, a washcloth, and a towel.

"There's no coming back for more. You lose something, that's your problem. You leave something somewhere and it's not there when you go back for it, that's your problem. Don't come crying to us. You lose your toothbrush or toothpaste, it's your teeth. If you lose your soap, you'll just have to walk around with a funky ass. Got it? Let's go."

They put me in a cell by myself for a week and I liked it. I was relaxing by myself in peace, especially since I didn't have to look over my shoulder all the time.

Suddenly at 2:00 in the morning while I was asleep, my cell door slid open and two guards rushed in and grabbed me.

"What's going on? What did I do?" I asked out of fear.

"Get up! Time to go!"

"Where are we going?"

"We're putting you in population."

They dragged me out of my cell and took me to C house. As we entered the new room, it was so quiet you could hear a pin drop. What made that even crazier is there were *400 people* in the room. There were hundreds of bunk beds side by side all the way down each row. I'll never forget that night. I knew from the second I got there that I would have no privacy and the area had the potential to be extremely dangerous.

I met this Muslim dude named Narco Corleone. He was locked up for 30 years – several years longer than I'd been on the earth.

He looked me over real quick. "Youngin', what you doing in here?"

Prison wisdom says whatever you told the judge, stick to your story. If you pleaded innocent in court, then don't admit guilt once you're locked up.

"*They* said I robbed a bank."

His eyes pierced my soul. "I'm going to give you one bit of advice. Don't take nothing from nobody, and don't take nothing from nobody. In other words, don't take any foolishness from anybody. Someone steps to you or disrespects you, handle it on the spot or they'll make your life a living hell for your whole bid."

"Okay."

"And when I say, 'and don't take nothing from nobody,' I'm talking about food or favors. Don't accept honey buns, candy bars, or anything else because that's the way they make you their woman. When you start receiving favors you can't give back, you're in trouble. Got it?"

"Got it."

We became the best of friends to the point where I had people on the outside writing to him to encourage him. He thought that was the best thing in the world because he never had anyone write to him before.

Narco didn't know what a bus or a train was. He'd been in there for 30 years. He missed out on so many worldly and technological advances; he was in complete awe at everything I told him. I'd tell him about VCRs, pagers, cell phones, tennis shoes, and drive-thru fast food restaurants that hand you your food while you're still in your car. He was amazed.

Narco always looked out for me and gave me instructions on prison rules. He was like my father figure. He got me my first job working in the kitchen. I needed that job badly. I cooked eggs on a tiny grill for thousands of inmates. I mean, I had crates of eggs stacked up 6-feet high and all I did all day long was cook eggs.

Bigs & Wigs

I was on my way to my first movie night. I didn't know what to expect. What type of movies do prisoners watch? Prison movies I guessed. But I was in for a major surprise. As I entered the area, I saw a man and a woman mauling each other like horny rabbits.

A huge smile spread across my face. I said to myself, *we can have girls up in this joint?! I'm with that. This is going to be easy*. I was so happy I didn't know what to do with myself. *Jail isn't going to be as hard as I thought it would be*, I thought. I began thinking about which of my ladies I was going to invite to come stay with me at Chateau Du Prison. But the closer I got to them, the more things began looking... funny, and not ha-ha funny. I mean 'what the hell?' funny. At around 5 feet away, I finally realized it was a dude kissing another dude with a wig on! They were getting it on like nobody was in there with them. All of my happiness turned to instant disgust and disappointment. I was destroyed. I couldn't even watch the movie.

I now know you can't judge whether a man is gay or not by looking at his size or his demeanor. These were some big, muscle-bound dudes kissing on men with wigs. And you won't know a thing until you walk up on it like I did. These weren't men that were tricked into being gay because they owed debts – no, these men wanted to do what they were doing. The ones wearing wigs were extra feminine and the horny men all over them probably missed being with a woman so much that they needed to release somehow just to keep from going crazy. If you weren't strong mentally, your mind could start playing tricks on you and you'd end up like them.

The worst part of this whole situation played itself out on visitation day. Those same guys that enjoyed messing with men in wigs would have their girlfriends and wives visit them. It was unbelievable! As I was in the visiting area, those same dudes would be kissing all over their women the same way they were kissing on those men in wigs. Those poor women had no clue where their boyfriends' or husbands' mouths had just been. I'd just shake my head.

Drugs On the Inside

I was tired of drinking water. I missed drinking fine wine and Hennessey. Thanks to Narco, he hooked me up with what prisoners call, homemade wine. And I drank lots of it. That first sip was like heaven because I hadn't tasted any type of flavor for the last two months. Homemade wine is so strong that before you finished your cup, your head would be spinning. You'd walk down the tier holding onto the bars hoping you could make it to your bunk.

There are more drugs in jail than on the streets. I'm serious. It didn't take me long to realize that drugs were everywhere. I pay attention to everything, and I figured out what was there, where it came from, who was running it, and, more importantly, how I could get me some.

I became friends with a great, big, body builder named Gregory. He had lots of weed, and if he liked you, you could hang around him and get high all day. Fortunately for me,

Gregory needed some help and presented me with the opportunity.

"Russell, I have a shipment of weed coming in tomorrow. You want to help me?"

I'm always interested in getting a piece of the action. "Yeah, man. What do you need?"

"During visitation, I need you to keep lookout for me and make sure the guards don't see what I have going on."

"You got it."

"Cool. Out of about 50 inmates and visitors, there will be only one or two guards. They normally lean against the walls and don't pay much attention to us unless we break the rules. The rule is that we can't hug or hold hands with our visitors, but they do allow us to kiss them. Just make sure one doesn't walk up on me, alright?"

"Alright."

Gregory had a white girl bringing drugs in little balloons. She would have them stuffed in her mouth when she entered the jail. The guards wouldn't check the women thoroughly because they didn't have but a few women guards, and the ones they had were not working the visitation area. The girl would lean over, kiss Gregory, transfer the balloons to him through the kiss, and then he would swallow them. He'd get at least 20 balloons by the end of the visit.

They strip-searched us after the visits. I'm talking about the searches that violate your manhood. They made us get naked, open our mouths, lift our tongues, bend over, spread our cheeks, and cough to make sure we didn't have any contraband. They'd never find anything because Gregory swallowed everything. When he got back to the cell, he'd throw it all up, clean the bags, and dry them. He'd then break all the bags open and put the weed in a shoe box.

There wasn't just weed in jail, there was also heroin. I saw one guy in jail die from the needle. Another dude on the tier shot some heroin and zoned out.

"Oh, man," he said to his friend. "This is some good dope," and nodded out.

His friend wasn't going to be left out. He took the needle out of his friend's arm and stuck it into his own arm, then he passed out, too. The first guy died, and the second guy was higher than Cootie Brown.

I started smuggling heroin into jail the same way Gregory smuggled in marijuana. Sometimes the guards brought in contraband. If you gave them $400, they'd bring you a whole ounce of weed, but you had to get the right guard. You had to get a guard you could talk to or manipulate. There was always somebody that was hungry for money. If you have the money, you can get an ounce of weed – no problem. It sounds backwards to people on the outside, but people would sell weed in jail to buy cigarettes. Cigarettes give you power in jail. Weed is nothing in jail, but cigarettes had power because everybody smoked cigarettes. And you couldn't buy cigarettes in jail. You had to have them shipped to you, and you're only allowed a certain amount. The max was a carton. And cigarettes were currency too. You could take a pack of cigarettes and buy two egg sandwiches. I worked in the kitchen and they'd let us leave with up to ten sandwiches. I'd take those sandwiches and buy cigarettes, then I'd trade the cigarettes for someone's commissary. There was a process to working the system, and I worked the hell out of it.

CHAPTER 6

Jack of All Jobs

Since I was an electrician by trade, I saw major opportunities to come up in the game. The kitchen was cool, and the egg hustle was okay, but I needed more. Plus, I liked to move around, and the kitchen had me in one spot all day. So I transferred out of the kitchen and into the electrical shop. I knew I'd excel because I was certified before being locked up. That's where I met my supervisor, Mr. Albeck. He was an electrician and he had his own company on the outside. His job was to take us around the jail fixing stuff. He quickly became impressed with me because I was fast and my work was top quality.

"Nice work, Russell."

"Thank you."

"Many people get transferred here and don't know what they're doing, but I see you're the real deal. How long have you been an electrician?"

"I've been one for a few years. I was working full-time when they threw me in jail."

"How much time do you have left to serve?"

"Hopefully less than ten years."

"Well, when you get out of jail, look me up. I'll give you a job."

He told me that every other month because I was rockin' and rollin' in there. I was in my element.

See, they didn't hire any outside people to fix anything in jail. If something broke or needed repair, they didn't call an electrician, plumber, or a welder because they had free labor – thousands of inmates. The 13th amendment of The Constitution of the United States clearly states "Neither slavery nor involuntary servitude, except as a punishment for crime whereof the party shall have been duly convicted." In laymen's terms, slavery can not exist in America unless a person has been convicted of a crime and sent to jail. Consequently, anything done by inmates in the state of MD was done for the state and that included laundry for the hospitals (inmates washed, dried, and folded washcloths, towels, and bed linen), the paint on the highways (inmates mix the chemicals and make the paint), the license plates on your cars and trucks were made by inmates, and all of the benches, desks, and office furniture used in state buildings were made in prison workshops. People think slavery doesn't exist, but the products created from it are all around them in government buildings, courtrooms, hospitals, on roads and highways, etc.

And electrical work isn't all that I did. I was a handy man, too. I'd do whatever job they had within my wheelhouse, and I was good at what I did. I fixed their doors. No one could fix them correctly but me. It got to the point where I became the go-to guy for certain jobs, and that brought major perks from the guards.

One example was during visitation. Everyone was allotted an hour with their visitors except for me and those that had connections.

"Alright! Times up!" the guards yelled. "Stand up, step back from your visitor, and line up at the door!"

I always did what they instructed, when they instructed, but things changed.

"You're good," the guard said under his breath as he stood next to me. "You have extra time. Go ahead and sit down."

Inmates live for letters, commissary, and visits. When he told me I had extra time, I was so excited, I almost cried! My friends who came to see me were used to leaving after an hour. Now, since I got the hookup, I'd keep them there for three hours.

They'd say, "Times up!" and my visitors would stand up to leave.

"Wait a minute," I'd say. "Relax. I have more time. I'm kind of important in here." My friends got tired of meeting with me for so long. They'd say, "Man, we've been here over two hours! That's too long. I have to go home." I understood. I just didn't want them to go.

Don't Call Me John

Being in jail makes you tense. You have to act extra tough and have your guards up all the time. So, getting a visit from a woman and letting your guard down for a moment felt good. There is nothing like being in the presence of a woman. I mean, looking into her eyes, smelling her, seeing her smile, and kissing her all over. Whoo! That made feel extra good.

My friend, Joyce, came to see me a lot. She was as sweet as a juicy peach, and I gave her all of me. We used to write each other and she was the woman that set up my buddy Narco with one of her buddies so that someone would write him.

One thing about Joyce was that she was very business smart, but had no common sense. She could solve a complicated math equation in her mind and explain the theory of relativity, but she couldn't last a second with a slickster. A stranger could ride up to her on a bicycle and ask her for $20 to take his mom to the emergency room and she'd naively give him the money.

I got her to bring some drugs to me like Gregory had women do for him. When she entered, I could see in her eyes that she was scared as a prostitute in church. I kissed her and swallowed the balloons she had, which wasn't many because she was new and extra nervous.

"Baby, I need you to have at least ten kisses for me tomorrow," I told her over the phone.

"I'll kiss you all you want, but I won't have the kind of kisses you want from me."

"Why not? What's wrong? They didn't give them to you?"

"I didn't go and get them because it didn't feel right. What if I got caught?"

"Baby, you didn't get caught last time, did you? Just do like you did and everything will be fine. Okay?"

But things weren't okay. She came, but she didn't have my balloons. That messed my money up because I had people looking forward to those drugs. I had to find another woman to bring me the drugs. Got to keep the customers happy.

But I was still crazy about Joyce because it wasn't just about the balloons with her. The next week, Joyce didn't make the trip to visit me. The following week I received a letter.

Dear Russell,

I love you so much with all of my heart. You have no idea how much I love you. You've taught me so much and I thank you for always being there for me. I couldn't visit you last week because I didn't want to tell you to your face what happened because I didn't want to hurt you because that would hurt me. It would be too emotional for me and I didn't want to cry in front of the other visitors. I met somebody else. He's a really nice guy. We have a lot in common, and we began dating. I'm so sorry, Russell, but we can no longer be together. I love you. Goodbye.

I was heartbroken. Crushed. I wasn't going to get any visits from the woman I loved
any more. Man, I was ready to kill somebody.

Russell Electric At Your Service!

Working for Mr. Albeck as an electrician was my job, but when he left, that's when my hustle began. I had lots of hustles going on. I would repair TVs, clocks, and anything electric that the inmates had. My biggest hustle was a goldmine. All I did was sit in my cell and hit the switch.

"Hey, what's that you got, Russell?" somebody called out to me.

"It's called Russell Electric. It gives you electricity 24-hours a day."

"Can you hook me up with Russell Electric?"

"I sure can."

"Man, I need those lights. How many will it cost?"

Before you knew it, I was hooking everybody up with electricity. All I had to do was get extra wires from my job every day and take them to my cell.

See, in prison, you don't control basic things like coming and going, getting something out of the refrigerator to eat, and cutting on the lights. We're all grown men, but when that clock struck midnight and the guard yelled, "Lights out!" they shut down the lights and electricity in all of the cells. The only people that had lights at night were the guards, and that's where I got paid. If someone wanted to watch TV, read a book, look at pictures, or whatever, he could just contact Russell Electric and I'd give him 24-hour electricity so he could see at night. They'd pay me cartons of cigarettes.

When the guards came, you'd turn the TV off. It worked fine until there was a shakedown. When that happened, the whole jail would be in lockdown position. Guards would come out of nowhere and make you stand outside the door of your cell. They'd tear it apart looking for contraband. All the wires I installed, they'd snatch them out. So inmates paid me all these cigarettes, and the guards snatched the wires out and shut down their lights and their TVs. So what did the inmates do? They paid me again to hook it back up for them. I hated shakedowns, but they were actually great for business.

Fight For My Life

I got big again in the joint like I was when I was on the streets selling 'water,' only this time I was selling cigarettes. I was like RJR Reynolds up in there. But when you get lots of money or attention, there's always somebody around the next corner that's going to try to take you down a peg or two. In prison, they play for keeps. When someone does something, they try to kill you because they don't want any witnesses or people coming after them.

I was in my cell fast asleep. Suddenly, I heard the door slide open. When they open one door, all of the doors open at the same time. For some reason, I didn't get up that morning to lock the door, and two dudes came in there, threw a cover over my head, and started shanking me. I hadn't done anything to anybody, but there they were trying to kill me. I think they set me up because they knew I had a nice hustle going on with hooking up people with electricity in their cells. They wanted to kill me and take all of my contraband.

Thank God they didn't have shanks that were really sharp and long. I could feel them, but they weren't really penetrating my skin deeply, but they were going in far enough for me! I went crazy on them dudes. I didn't have a shank to fight back – all I had was the TV my father sent me. I fought to get the sheet from over my head, then I picked the TV up and hit one dude over the head with it. The other guy ran, and the one I hit got up and ran. Before I could chase them, the cell locked. I wasn't hurt badly, but they knocked out my two front teeth.

The guards sent me to the infirmary so the scrapes and gashes could be disinfected. Afterwards, they took me to my cell and cornered me.

"Who attacked you?" they asked.

"I don't know."

"How did they look?"

"I don't know."

"Are they in this area?"

"I don't know?"

"Do you know anything about them?"

"I don't know who did it." I knew exactly who did it, but I wasn't going to tell them because in prison, snitches get stitches.

"Don't be scared."

"I'm not scared."

"If you're afraid they're going to attack you again, we'll put you in protective custody."

"I don't know anything."

They got really mad at me. "Fine! Tell us or we're going to put you in solitary confinement. Is that you want? You won't be able to leave your cell nor have any contact with anybody."

"I don't care," I said. "Do what you have to do."

They locked me in my cell for a week and didn't let me come out for anything. Not telling gave me a lot of respect. I knew that it was some dudes from DC that stabbed me up, but I wanted to take care of things my own way. After that week was up, I made a few deals with the right people and went about my usual business. Those dudes didn't know what hit them. My people robbed them and beat the hell out of them. They ended up in PC (Protective Custody). Payback ain't a snitch – it's a mean bitch.

CHAPTER 7

A Taste of Freedom

In accordance with my contract, I had six months to do on work release. They gave me a choice to work in a saw mill or Roy Rogers. I figured I'd work at Roy Rogers because they had food and I could eat. I was excited on my first day there because all I could dream about since I found out I would be working there was eating something other than prison food. When I bit into my first burger and fries…man, you couldn't tell me nothing! Roy Rogers made the best burgers in the history of burgers. I died and went to the big 'Upper Room' in the sky. The soda capped things off. I was still an inmate, but I got a taste of freedom, and it was damn good.

There was a young, white woman working there from Tennessee. She lived in the backwoods of a small city and had never seen a black person before – she heard of them, but never saw one in person. When she came in, she was kind of different, so I began talking to her. She was the manager, but I wasn't intimidated. And since I was a city guy, I knew I could get her with ease.

"You know who you remind me of?"

"Who?"

"You're like June Cleaver on *Leave It to Beaver*."

"Why do you say that?"

"Because you dress all prim and proper. You know what? I'm going to name you June."

She blushed and laughed.

"I'm serious. You're going to be June, and I'm going to be Ward. All of these other people working here are our kids, The Beave and Wally."

I started dating her while on work release. She would get hotel rooms for us all the time. And just like I was happy to sink my teeth into that fast food after eating prison food for years – after not having sex for years, I was happy to sink myself into her. We'd have wild, crazy sex for hours and then after our sex-capades she would bring me back to prison. She was responsible for me because I was in her custody since she was the manager. I saw her years after I got released. I yelled to her, "June Cleaver!" She looked at me and with a big smile on her face immediately shouted back, "Ward!" She never forgot me.

My cousin came to visit me one weekend. After catching up on what's going on with the fam and the hood, I told him I'd be getting out soon and asked him if he'd seen Joyce.

"No, but Russell, I want you to meet this nice girl when you get out. Maybe y'all can hook up."

"Who is she and where do you know her from?"

"Her sister is dating my brother. I think you'll like her."

"Okay. That's cool with me."

"I'll set it up so you can meet her when you get home. You're going to like her. Trust me."

Days later, as I was heading to the pre-release unit, I saw this pretty thang walk by. She stopped me dead in my tracks. She was there to see somebody else, but that didn't stop me from staring at her. There was something extra special about her. I said to myself, *that's a nice looking shawty right there,* but I never saw her at the prison again. I had no idea she was going to be the love of my life.

Graduating Prison

I made it through prison by being strong. I prayed no matter what was going on. Every night, I got on my knees and thanked God Almighty for keeping safe that day. It's something my grandmother instilled in me back when I was little. To this day, I thank the Lord for putting me through what He put me through. It taught me lessons I definitely couldn't have learned on my own.

Another thing that helped me make it through prison was minding my own business. I always stayed to myself unless I was making deals and hustling. I also took Narco's advice and always used it.

I thought I knew it all before I went in, but I came out smarter and slicker than ever before. I learned how to smuggle drugs into the prison. I learned how to manipulate the prison system, and I learned how to manipulate people even better. By having so many jobs and being around so many different types of people, it allowed me to better learn and observe where people were coming from and where they were going. It was time for me to leave and I was ready to get back to life on the outside.

From the Bottom Up

After five years in the penitentiary, I came home to nothing. The woman I gave access to my house took everything. I still had the townhouse that I was paying on, but all of my furniture, clothes, shoes, and mink coats were gone. I guess she thought I would be gone for seventeen years, but I was out in five. I didn't even waste time getting mad at her. My immediate goal was to get a new place, which I did, and get it furnished. My new place was going to look a hundred times better than my old place.

One thing she left, which was of great value to me, was my cocaine cane. I always set it in the corner, and when I got out, it was right where I left it.

I didn't have a car, so my brother let me use his big Lincoln until I got on my feet. I only drove to important places because that sucker guzzled gas like a fat kid slurping a Slurpee. Every time I drove by a gas station the car said, "Momma, thirsty."

I had transportation, but I had no furniture, no clothes, and no money. The plan was to get a job, and start selling 'water' again–that would allow me to buy clothes and a new car--but I wasn't going to buy furniture. I was going to steal it. Why buy something I could get for free?

I didn't find a PCP connect that I could buy 'water' from, so I only bought dust to smoke, and I smoked a lot with my brother. The only connect I had was powder cocaine, so I started selling that. I began hanging with Bob, who was the owner of a carpet business. He'd let me do jobs with him and that's how I made a few dollars. It turns out Bob did coke and he liked my bartering idea. We were on a job at a fancy store and saw a nice waterbed, and I had to have it.

"Bob, I want that water bed." I pulled out some cocaine. "This should be enough to get it for me."

Bob looked the amount over, took it, and put it in his pocket.

"Hold on," I said. "I also want those sheets, pillowcases, and pillows."

I brought that waterbed home, filled that sucker up with water, and had that thing rocking whenever I had women over. But when you were on it when you were high, you'd be like, "Make it stop!" On top of that, the silk sheets would make you slide off of the bed, especially when that dust had you thinking you were lost at sea or being washed down a river. The waterbed brought a new experience to being high on that dust.

Jail Mate

I was out of prison about six months when I finally met the woman my brother was trying to set me up with when I was about to be released. I went to her sister's house to pick her up, and low and behold, it was the same woman that caught my attention when she was walking by in the prerelease unit! This was definitely a sign. I knew she was extra special and was going to be my baby because it was love at first sight. Her name was Kathy, and she reminded me of a school teacher because of her sweet, studious demeanor. She had little glasses, stockings, and a little fro.

We went on a date in my brother's Lincoln. First, I took her to my place and cooked dinner for her. I knew my fried chicken and potatoes would impress her a little bit, and if it didn't, I knew my clean, fancy bathroom, my floor model TV, and nice furniture would. I even had a Christmas tree of my own for the first time. After we ate dinner, I took her to the movies, then we came back to my place.

When women came to my place, they would always come in and say, "Wow. You're doing pretty good. Your house is really nice and neat." I set the trap and they took the bait every time. I had cooked Kathy dinner, took her to the movies, showed her my fancy apartment, and even let her see my waterbed with the silk sheets. And don't you know this woman wouldn't give me none. Zero. Nil. Zilch. ! I couldn't believe it. I was like, *What's wrong with this woman?* Everybody that I baited gave it up, but not her. I kept sweet talking her trying to change her mind into the early hours of the morning.

Around 2:00 in the morning, a woman named Pamela came over unannounced. I messed around with her a little, but she wasn't my girlfriend or anything like that. Anyway, she came over in a cab looking for a favor from me. I didn't think nothing of allowing her in and giving her a few dollars because I just met Kathy that day. It wasn't a big deal to me. I let her in and took her into the kitchen.

"What's up?" I asked her. "What's going on?"

"I need a favor. Something came up and I need some money."

"Okay. How much?"

"You got $50?"

The next thing I know, Kathy stormed in from around the corner.

"Who in the hell is this asking you for money?"

"Who am I?" Pam yelled. "Who are you?"

"Relax, Pam, I got this. Kathy, this is my old girlfriend," I said.

Kathy spewed, "Your girlfriend? Oh, no! You ain't giving her nothing!"

"You aren't even my girlfriend. What are you talking about?"

"Yeah," Pam said. "Now mind your damn business!"

Kathy gave Pam a mean look and then looked at me. "She better get the fuck out of here."

Pam didn't move, so Kathy went and got my cane. I shoved Pam toward the door.

"Go, go, go," I told Pam as I put a bill in her hand.

Pam looked in her hand. "This is only $10. I need $50."

"That's all I have. That's enough to get you home." I closed the door and looked at Kathy. "You must think you're my girlfriend for real."

She rolled her eyes and put the cane down.

We just met less than 24 hours ago and she was acting like that. I quickly realized she was a bossy person. Things simmered down and got back to how they were before Pam showed up. We talked a little more and even kissed. Right before the sun rose; she stood and grabbed her coat.

"I'm going home now."

"Huh?" She was still leaving without giving me none. I never had a girl do that to me before. I wasn't used to a woman turning me down. I took her home and that was that.

She turned me down for about a month. I said to myself, *what the hell? Something must be wrong with this girl.* There wasn't. She just wasn't like the other girls I brought home. She made me wait. And I waited.

Kathy moved in with me five months later. Right before meeting Kathy, I started going through a slump because the effects of the dust started kicking in. So, when she and I began dating seriously, my hustle slowed down even more. My life was about to change because I was in love with Kathy and in love with getting high. What was I going to do?

CHAPTER 8

Just Place Your Order

I hung out with a guy named Gunny who was a mechanic and a hustler. He knew how to wire trucks quickly without damaging the casing of the steering column. He was the best at stealing Fords. He knew them so well inside and out; he taught us how they worked in case we ever needed to steal them on our own. And we needed big trucks to pull off what we were doing. He would drive around searching for the perfect truck to steal and then he'd steal it. Afterwards, we'd take the truck back to the same exact parking place and park it exactly where it was, give or take a few inches. Why did we take it back and park it like that? Because we'd go back two or three days later and get the same truck which we'd already wired and had set up. We'd take the same truck, go back out on a heist, then park it again. This went on for a long time. Until this day, they never connected that truck to any of the burglaries or robberies we did because it was still sitting in the same parking place every morning when they got there and every night when they left. That was genius of us, wasn't it?

Gunny had a brother named Sugarboy that was good at setting everything up. Sugarboy was a criminal mastermind, and he had eyes and ears everywhere. Anything that went on in the streets, you can best believe Sugarboy knew about it before it happened. Sometimes he'd have me sit in the car with him and act like I was doing something as he observed a location to figure out its weaknesses. He would find opportunities, figure out a way to come up on some money or products, then devise a plan to steal it.

Sugarboy organized crews to do the jobs, but he'd never go on the jobs. Not only was he smart enough to not get his hands dirty, but he was smart enough to hire the right people and create airtight plans. We'd go over the plan together, steal what he sent us to steal, and bring everything to him. He'd sell everything and give us a cut of the money.

Eventually, so many people began asking me for appliances and furniture that I began doing stuff on the side. People would come up to me.

"Russell, I just bought a house. I need a refrigerator."

"What kind and color?"

"My kitchen is brown, so can you get me a beige one?"

"I can get you any color you want. I can get you one with the freezer at the top and the fridge at the bottom or one with two doors that has the freezer on the left and the fridge on the right. Do you want an ice maker where you put your cup on the button and ice comes out?"

"You got those?"

"I can get you one."

"How soon?"

"If you got the money, I can get it to you tonight."

People came to me for refrigerators, gas stoves, electric stoves, dishwashers, washing machines, dryers, microwaves, sofas. You name it, I got it for them. All they had to do was tell me the color, and I'd bring the exact thing they wanted to their doorstep that night – and I'd use the same truck Gunny wired.

A Model Thief

Our main hustle was breaking into model homes. If there was a new, fancy development selling houses, you can best believe we were there. We'd tour houses in Maryland, DC, and Virginia to see which ones were worthy of being hit because we had precise orders.

We'd look inside the home first, then that night we'd go in the door and see if the alarm went off. If it went off, we'd see if the police would show up. We'd give them half an hour to 45 minutes. If they didn't show up, we'd back the truck up to the house, go inside, and tear the place apart. We'd take everything out, and I mean everything. Then we'd close the door and disappear into the night. It got easier and easier. If the landscaping was nice, I took the flowers out the yard and sold those, too. Do you remember "The Grinch That Stole Christmas?" Well, I was the Grinch that stole the whole damn house.

There was so much nice furniture that I would change furniture at my leisure. If I saw something that was nicer than what I had, or if I just wanted something different, I'd get rid of my "old" new furniture in exchange for something newer. It got to the point where I was changing furniture every six months. I never told people the truth. Whenever somebody got nosey about where I got my furniture, I'd tell them I bought everything on credit cards.

I'd get a woman to go with me just to make it look like we were a couple. We'd get dressed up, act like we're looking to buy a new home, and get a tour of model homes. It was so much fun that I would use different aliases and even different accents. The plan was simple: go inside with huge smiles on our faces, take notes of everything of value, and make a note of where they were located. We'd go through the entire house, including the basement if they had one. One would talk and distract the person showing us the house while the other would take precise notes down to the doors and windows in the home. I wanted the notes to be so good that we could walk inside in total darkness and know where certain items were located.

"Good afternoon, and welcome to Ryan Estates. I'm David Hamilton. And you are?"

"We're Mr. and Mrs. Burrell. This place is lovely."

"I'm glad you like it. Hopefully we can make one of these your new home."

"That would be nice."

"Everything is state of the art in these homes. I can just you see you getting ice from this stainless steel refrigerator's ice machine and then having your glass cleaned by this stainless steel dishwasher? Can't you see these appliances being yours?"

"I sure can," I said smiling like a Cheshire cat. What he didn't know was that by the end of the day, those appliances were going to be mine, and he's going to be filling out a police report in the morning.

This one house we came across was *my house*. I wasn't doing this one for Sugarboy or anybody else – this baby was mine all the way. It had the perfect art paintings on the wall, my favorite kind of carpet and the right color, the exact dining room set I wanted, I mean, this place had the whole nine yards. They were prepared, too, because the place had a serious alarm system. Unfortunately for them, I was knew how to bypass the alarm.

When my partner had the attention of the salesman, I opened a window, taped a piece of cigarette paper over the top of the sensor on the window, and then pulled the window back down without locking it. Problem solved. We then left to look at more model homes.

When the sun set, I took the Gunny and Sugarboy to the special house and chilled in the woods until everybody inside left for the day. I didn't bother trying breaking in through the front door this time.

"Gunny," back the truck up, I instructed.

"Didn't you say it had an alarm? I'll be ready as soon as you break in the door."

"Just back it up into the driveway," I said. Then I looked to all three of the guys. "I have the alarm taken care of. But on this one, we're going to do things different on this one. We're all going to go in through the window and move all the furniture and appliances to the front door. Once I open the door, we're moving everything out in less than 15 minutes."

They didn't think it would work, but I knew it would. I ran across the street and went through the window. When the truck stopped, each one of them came through the window. We carefully took all of my things to the front door including the carpet. That's right, I brought my box cutter, cut the carpet at the walls, and carried that baby to the front door. I then unlocked the door and looked at them.

"Y'all ready?" I asked.

When they said they were, I pulled the door open and we rock and rolled as the alarm blared. See, if we tripped the alarm and waited across the street and the police showed up and then the salesman came, there was a chance I wasn't going to get what I wanted, and I didn't want to take that chance because these appliances and furniture were mine. We ended up packing the stuff into the moving truck so fast that we were done in 10 minutes flat!

I was now sitting pretty in my newly furnished apartment. I wanted to thank the interior designer that decorated the model home because he or she actually decorated my place.

A Voice From Above

I was sitting in my apartment depressed. I got my first real job since being out of prison – a head electrician supervising ten guys – and I was working like a runaway slave on the job. I was depressed from all the stress, and whenever I felt bad, the first thing I wanted to do was get high. The truth was that the slightest thing made me want to get high. I said to myself, *I need a good joint*, and I knew I had a joint of angel dust in the freezer. It was in there for two weeks, and the longer it sits, the stronger it gets. I fired that baby up, took about three puffs, and my whole head split wide open. I started talking to the Lord.

"Lord, what is going on in my life? Tell me what I should do."

The Lord talked back to me and said, "You don't need that waterbed."

I was high out of my mind. I went and got a knife and stabbed the waterbed to death. Water gushed everywhere, but the Lord wasn't done.

"You don't need that TV, either."

I took a step back, POW! -- I kicked a hole in the TV. I ripped all the blinds down in the kitchen, then began ripping the entire place apart. I picked up something, probably the TV, and threw it at the balcony window and knocked it off its hinges. Then I walked through the glass and on to the balcony.

People were smoking in the parking lot below. I looked down on them like I was God.

"All y'all are going to hell!" I yelled. "You're going to hell for smoking those cigarettes! Look at cha!"

They looked at me like I was crazy. I'm high on dust and I had the nerve to get on them about smoking cigarettes. That dust had me losing my mind. I went off on every man, woman, and child out there.

"Get out of here!"

"Your high ass better not jump off that balcony!" somebody yelled.

"Don't worry about me, worry about yourselves! God is coming back to get all y'all!"

"Shut the hell up and go back inside!"

"No, I ain't going inside!"

I heard police sirens and I went back inside.

The high instantly went away. That's when I noticed my place was destroyed. When I heard that heavy police knock pounding on my door, I opened it, got on my knees, and put my hands behind my back.

"Lord, help me!" I pleaded with my head to the sky because I didn't want to die. I just knew the police were going to shoot and kill me because that's what they always did to people on PCP.

Instead of shooting me, they handcuffed me and took me to a psychiatric hospital. They had me handcuffed to the bed and would not let me go anywhere.

Now sober, I asked the cops, "Can I leave now?"

"We're not going to let you out until you pee."

"I ain't gotta pee," I protested.

See, they knew I was on some type of drug and they wanted to get some of my urine to see what drug I was on. I didn't want to scare Kathy away, so I called my sister instead. She eventually came up there to rescue me.

"Thank you for taking care of him," she said with love in her heart. "I'll take it from here."

"Ma'am, we can't let him go because he destroyed property and he's under the influence."

"But he destroyed his own property. Look, if you let him go, I'll take him home with me."

God bless my sister. They don't usually do it, but they let me go into her custody. I avoided jail, but I returned home to eviction papers.

CHAPTER 9

Kathy's Father

I was head over heels for Kathy. I even began going to church with her. After leaving church, we'd stop by her parents' house to spend a little time with her family and shoot the breeze. Kathy was very close with her family and there was no way I could be her boyfriend without spending extensive time with her family.

Her father liked me a lot. He thought I was a nice church boy that could do no wrong. He was right about me being nice and being a church boy, but I did plenty of things that were illegal. Nevertheless, her father couldn't tell how I really was because I didn't wear my criminal actions on my sleeve. After all, I was going to church almost every Sunday and showing up to his house in a nice suit. I was also taking his daughter with me, and his daughter wouldn't date a bad guy, right? He didn't know that his daughter was with a straight up criminal – a nice criminal, but still a criminal. I remember one particular time we were talking after church.

"Hey, Russell. How are you doing?"

"I'm doing fine."

"How was service?"

"It was excellent. The pastor preached a very good sermon. The choir was good, too."

"You know what, Russell? You're going to be a preacher one day."

"A preacher? Why do you say that?"

"I can just feel it. There's something about you that's Godly and refined."

I appreciated that comment. I prayed every day and went to church, but I was far from a preacher.

I was over there one time and I told Kathy I was going to make a run over a friend's house and I'd be back in an hour. Her father asked to go with me just to get out of the house. Anyway, I went to my buddy's house, and it just so happened that Kathy's cousin was there. He rolled up on Kathy's father, which was his uncle.

"What are you doing here?" he asked her father.

"I came here with Kathy's boyfriend."

"Who?"

"Him right over there," he said as he pointed to me.

"That's Kathy's boyfriend? I know him. That's the biggest dope dealer in the area."

After that day, her father kicked me to the curb. He didn't have much of anything to say to me from that point forward. In his eyes, I was the bad guy that was dating his daughter. I don't blame him for not liking me.

I Can Make It Better

Despite Kathy being a straight-laced church girl and a strong sister with 'around the way' qualities, she was the coolest wife a man could ask for. But like every other wife in the world, she was about that 50/50, "what's yours is mine and what's mine is mine" marriage. And I was a crackhead. So...

Kathy:

Russell always left me in the apartment by myself and I was sooo bored. There was nothing on TV, but there was water in the freezer. I dabbled in weed and dust a tiny bit, and so I said to myself, *I'm going to make some dust better than Russell.* I put some parsley flakes in a bottle, poured a little 'water' on it, and mixed it up. I didn't know how much should be on it, I just put the amount I thought looked good.

Hmm-hmm, I thought to myself as I added more and more 'water,' *this is going to be good.* I put the dust in foil, then put it in the freezer to sit. I tried to let it sit, but I was too anxious to see how it turned out because it was calling my name a little bit. I got it out, rolled it in some paper, smoked it, and it was a wrap – I was instantly high out of my mind. I got paranoid and scared, so I grabbed the Bible and clutched it tightly with both hands. Then I sat in the chair frozen.

I kept saying to myself, *Lord, if You let me come down off this high, I'll never do it again.*

Russell:

I came home to find Kathy sitting on the couch frozen like an old Negro woman statue. She had the strangest look on her face, one that I've seen a million times on people's faces. The part that threw me off was the fact that I knew I didn't leave any dust there.

I said, "Kathy, what did you do?"

Kathy broke out of her frozen state and started giggling. "I made my own stuff. I didn't want that old weak stuff y'all got."

"How did you make it?"

"I put some 'water' from the freezer on some parsley flakes and mixed it up."

I looked at the bottle and saw a lot of 'water' missing. She made the dust too strong. I said, *Is you coo-coo for Cocoa Puffs?!* When dust has too much 'water' added to it, whoever smokes it zaps out – and Kathy was Roger Troutman-zapped!

"I have to go to church!" she yelled. "Come on! Let's go to church!"

I shook my head. "It's okay, baby. Hold on." I poured a glass of milk for her to drink. That was the quickest way I knew of to bring her high down. As I watched her guzzle the milk down, I started to understand why her father had it out for me. I wasn't good for his daughter. After looking at her zoning out into another galaxy, he may have been right. Father's know best, right?

CHAPTER 10

The Crack Is Coming!

I was hanging out with my buddy Earnest, and there were some dudes around snorting cocaine. I brought up smoking dust, but Earnest flipped the script.

"Man, you gotta try this new thing called crack."

"Ain't no needles involved, is it?"

"No, there's a pipe. What you do is take a pipe, put a little bit of crack in it, light it, and inhale it." I got some. Hold on."

"Cool."

He had everything right there. I watched closely as he put the crack in the pipe, lit it, and inhaled. He looked like he was in paradise. Then he handed it to me.

"You want to try it?"

"Yeah, I'll try it," I said as I lit the pipe and inhaled.

He stared into my eyes. "How does it feel? Do you feel anything?"

"I don't feel nothing."

"Do it again."

I lit it like before, inhaled deeply, and blew the smoke out.

"Do you feel it?"

"Not yet."

"No, you would already feel something because it hits you in seconds. You're not doing it right."

We passed it back and forth, and eventually I inhaled the smoke, swallowed it, held it, and then let it go.

"DING-DONG! DING-DONG!" is all I could hear, but Earnest's voice squeezed through the noise.

"Do you feel anything?"

"I don't know if I feel anything, but what are those bells?"

"Oh, you did it right!" Earnest said with excitement.

Loud bells were literally ringing in my head. It felt so good that I kept smoking nonstop that day. I didn't even go home. The high only lasts three or four minutes, so you have to keep doing it if you want to stay high. I went to sleep, woke up, and started doing it some more. I was officially a crack addict and I didn't even know it. I never heard the bells again, but I kept smoking crack trying to hear them. Everyone that smokes crack does so with hopes of feeling the way they did the first time they took a hit – but all they are really doing is chasing the bells.

Chef Russell

Smoking freebase cocaine was a hassle, and it never picked up. When it was discovered you could cook coke and make crack, it was so much more convenient for people to smoke. I began cooking cocaine to make crack. I'd take a big rock and smoke it in an hour or two. The good coke would make you take one hit and say, "Wooh! I have to sit back for a minute."

Ernest taught me how to cook crack really good. We started making our own because we were buying from people that put too much cut on the cocaine, so we weren't getting a good high (a cut is added to stretch the batch to increase profit). When we started making it, we knew exactly what we had because we snorted a little to find out how strong it was – that told us how much cut to put on it. You don't want to cut it too much because it would be too weak, and that would weaken your sales and reputation. The legendary drug dealer, Rayful Edmond, was selling the good stuff because he was getting quality cocaine and putting the perfect cut on it.

I'd go to the liquor store and buy a real pipe made of glass and I'd buy a pack of cigarettes for the ashes. I needed ashes to filter the coke when I smoked so it wouldn't drain so fast.

Pipe Life

A crack high is a big rush. A rush like you've never felt before. It hits you extremely hard and takes you to a place beyond the planets like no other. The problem though, is that it only lasts two or three minutes. 180 seconds of pure joy. If you get a really good hit, it may last four minutes.

But that kind of joy comes at a price. Now what makes crack different from other drugs like PCP and snorting cocaine is that those drugs didn't stop me from dressing in fancy clothes, buying a nice car, and taking care of my home. On those, I could go to work, take care of home, sing in the church choir, and smoke it on nights and weekends when I had free time. But on crack, I became 'Barry The Bum.' It takes control of your life and your every thought. I had 'do crack' at the top of my to-do list all the time and everything under that had no hope of getting done. I didn't have time to clean anything. Instead, my time was devoted to figuring out how much money I had, where the dealer was, and how fast I could get to him so I could get another hit.

Everything I did was geared toward getting high, and that includes working. I had a job, but even while I was there, all I could think about was getting high. When I got paid on Friday, I didn't want to lift a finger to work because my incentive to work was gone. I had money for crack, what did I need to go back to work for? But by Sunday night, I'd be out of money, and I was suddenly motivated to work again... for more crack.

I remember Kathy seeing a friend of ours smoking.

"You know what, Russell?" she said with a frown. "I know people that smoke crack every day and I don't see how they can do drugs that much."

The next thing you know, Kathy was smoking crack every day. This was a hardworking woman that took great care of herself and had lots of discipline, but crack overpowered her good qualities like it does to everyone that puts their lips to that glass. Crack breaks down the strongest people with no problem, and our lives and everything around us started spiraling downward fast.

Kathy and I were different kinds of smokers. She could smoke a little bit, chill, then smoke a little more later. I, on the other hand, smoked rock, after rock, after rock. Whatever I had, I was going in on it. If you line up two rocks, I'm smoking both. If you line up ten rocks, I'm smoking all ten. There was no chill in me.

One time, I was in the bathroom by myself getting high and it felt like my heart was trying to jump out my body. I thought I was dying! But I never put the pipe down. I fell on the floor from the pain and still had the pipe in my hand. When I got up, I said to myself, "Wow! I need to hit some more of this." That's how good it was. That's how the addiction of crack is. Once a person gets hooked, it's hard to stop. And there are many kinds of addictions: food addiction, alcoholism, nicotine addiction from cigarettes, reality TV addictions, plastic surgery addictions. What makes being addicted to crack different from all others is that crack actually calls to you. I'm serious. The voice is so loud that it's as if someone is next to you talking. Sleep isn't much of a help because you'll have crack dreams. Crack reminds me of Freddy Kruger from the movie *"Friday The 13th"* – it's going to get you as soon as you close your eyes and drift off. There's no escaping crack once you hit that pipe.

The Zombie Next Door

LaTonya, Kathy and I's next-door neighbor was really cool. She'd come over sometimes when I was on my lunch break and get high. She only smoked weed and love boat. I was on my lunch break like any other day, and she came out her door.

"What are you about to do, Russell?"

"Get high real quick."

"On what?"

"What you think?" I said because I knew she knew the answer already. "Crack."

"Can I try it?"

"Come on."

I got my pipe, some crack, and a lighter, and then took my time showing her how to do it. I fired that baby up and got sky high. She just watched. When the high came down, I went to the bathroom to pee. When I came out the bathroom a minute later, she was passed out on the floor.

The woman was dead! I didn't know how to do CPR or anything, so I panicked. I didn't want to call the police because that would land me in jail. All that I could think to do was get towels and ice to put on her head to revive her. I went back and forth for 30 minutes getting more ice, cold water, and anything I could to revive her, but she wouldn't wake up. I was scared out of my mind. *I ain't never killed nobody*! I picked the phone up with my trembling hands and dialed a number.

"Hey, Tony. I'm going to get back late from my break."

"You sound strange. You okay?"

His statement scared me even more because now Tony could testify that he heard me talking strangely. I had to be short with him.

"Cover for me. Bye."

As I tried to figure out what to do next, I heard something move. I looked over and saw Latonya sitting up like a zombie.

"Are you okay?" I asked as I helped her to her feet.

She didn't say anything. She nodded and walked out the door. I made sure she went into her apartment, and then I went into mine, closed the door, and fell to the floor right where she was lying two minutes ago. "Thank you, God!!!"

Working High to 5

I was an excellent electrician and supervisor until I got on crack. I tried to fight it, but it was TKOing me every day like what Merriweather did to McGregor. I'd have my guys working while I was in my office getting high all day long. I'd go down and check on my guys to make sure everything was alright, then beeline back into my office and smoke some more crack. They knew I was getting high. My eyes would be crack-shot red. I'd have this crazy, deranged look in my eyes and my clothes would be disheveled and musty. Anybody that knew me could clearly see I looked different, but I didn't care. My appearance wasn't important at all.

Lawman was my coworker and right-hand man. He smoked crack, too, and we used to get high together. As soon as the shift began and the crew had their duties, I'd look to Lawman.

"Lawman, come on up to the office," I'd tell him. "We need to discuss your assignment." I'd make up reasons every other day. Once again, we weren't fooling anybody. He'd step into my office, lock the door, and roll his sleeves up.

The cigarette lighter got so weak one time, we went and got a small blow torch. Maann, those rocks burned so good with that torch, I ended ordering a blow torch just for my office. When we finished, Lawman would leave the office looking the same way I looked, and he hadn't done an ounce of work.

Eventually, the jobs I was supervising started falling apart. We fell so far behind that the company called a guy out to come assist me. He ended up taking over my job as supervisor. Smoking crack got me demoted. You'd think that demotion was a wake-up call, right? It wasn't. I kept getting high.

I'd call into work and tell them I'm going to be late just so I could smoke crack. Then I started calling in sick. Then I stopped going in all together, because I was up all night smoking crack. My job gave me every chance in the world, but all I wanted to do was smoke crack. Crack became my new full-time job.

CHAPTER 11

Jamaican Me High

One day, Kathy came barging through the door, "Russell! Russell! I came out of my bedroom with my bat ready to do my best Sammy Sosa impression against somebody's head. But nobody was there. I said, "What's wrong with you? She said, "I was down at the Chinese food place ordering some food when I heard these Jamaicans talking while they were waiting for their food. Okay, I said. She continued on, "I checked out their car outside. They're loaded. They were smoking blunts and talking loud and stuff, when one of them says, "Wen de shipment come?" The other answers, "Tree-tirty, Ras." I said, "Shipment of what? Bongs, Clark shoes, Bob Marley records?" "Crack, stupid!" I scowled, "Jamaicans selling crack? "You don't believe me? she said. They're staying at the apartment up the street. Come on!" I looked at my Kathy. She 'd gone from church-girl to crack robber…

She took me to the apartment, and sure enough, they were there just as she said. She devised the plan. We were going to observe them closely to see where they were slipping and then rob them. Oh, by the way, we didn't have any money. We had that 'crack-idence.' That's the false confidence crack gives you to do the stupidest superhuman crimes. Kathy knocked on the apartment door to talk to the Jamaicans while I broke into the guy's car to steal his radio. When they came out, Kathy saw me taking the radio and made me stop.

"What are you doing?" she asked me as I ducked between the cars.

"I almost had his radio. Why didn't you keep talking to them so I could get it?"

"Forget that stupid radio. They have a suitcase full of drugs!

"What are they about to do?"

"They're heading to Tony's house to do business with him."

When we got to Tony's house, they all went into a back room to talk. "Russell," Kathy whispered, "go outside and come back in through the window. I'm going to leave it open for you." She then went into the back room with them.

They left the back room, and a man named Jerry led them downstairs to let Tony sample the drugs. Kathy was the last person to leave the room. That was my cue, so I walked to the door.

"Jerry and Kathy, I'll be back in 20 minutes. Fellas," I said to the Jamaican guys, "it was nice meeting you."

I left the house as they headed down to the basement. I sprinted around the back, climbed through the window, found the suitcase and opened it. Inside, there were huge crack rocks shaped like pancakes, and a bag of money. I took $400, a handful of pancake rocks, and climbed out the window. I went up the street, stashed the loot, waited 5 minutes, then came back to the house.

"I'm ready," I said to the Jamaicans. "What y'all got? I got $200."

They hooked me up at bargain crack prices. From then on, I hung around Tony's house a lot because he always had crack for sale. He sold drugs, but he didn't have any transportation. That's where my truck came in handy. He'd give me a rock and take my truck. He also gave me a little corner in his basement, which was blocked off by a sheet hanging from the ceiling. I went down there and got high for days off of their money and their crack, and they never even knew it!

Kathy was visiting with me on an occasion where Tony took my truck. She and I smoked the little rock he gave us in a few minutes, and that's when we began figuring out how to get more.

Kathy said, "He can't take all the crack with him. It has to be around here somewhere?"

She's a genius, I thought. "It must be in the safe."

"Can you get into it?" she asked.

"I can if I have enough time."

"Hurry up! I'll keep look out."

We bumped fists and said, "Crack Twin powers activate!" She said, "Form of an owl." I said, "Shape of a lock picker." Yes, crack made us think we were the Super Twins from the *Superfriends* cartoons on Saturday mornings. I raced upstairs to pick the safe. Once I found it, I kneeled, put my ear against the spin-lock and started turning it. *I couldn't hear a damn thing!* My heart was racing too loud, and it looked so easy on TV. Thinking quick on my feet, instead of trying to pick the lock, I decided to take the pins out the safe and pry it open from the opposite side of the lock, but my super crack strength wasn't working!

"They're coming!" Kathy said.

I rushed to put the pins back, but I couldn't. Kathy pushed me out of the window. We climbed out, jumped to the ground, and hauled ass!

"Russell!" I heard Tony yell from the bedroom window behind us. But by then, I was two houses away running as fast as I could. I left my truck and everything that was in my little area of the basement. A few days later, I crept back to his house in the middle of the night and got my truck and another pancake rock. Sorry, Tony. Respect.

Crack Calls

Crackheads have good intentions. They're in their right minds most of the time, but crack overpowers their sane thoughts and taunts them. I had a major crack addiction, but I knew the bills had to be paid. I'd get paid and set money aside for rent. I budgeted all of the money, including how much I would spend on crack, and then I'd rush to the dealer, get what I needed, and got busy smoking the second I got back home. The problem was the crack didn't last as long as my weekend. I smoked all Friday night, but I had to figure out a way to get enough crack to smoke Saturday and Sunday. I'd sit there pondering, and then the crack would begin talking audibly. Seriously, no joke. My crack actually called me. I heard the phone ring. I answered.

Russell. Russell.

What do you want, Crack?

I just want to remind you that there's plenty more of me right down the street. Your local crack representative won't be out there all night.

But I'm out of money.

You have the money you budgeted for your bills.

I can't spend that.

Sure you can. You'll get it back before the first of the month. Now go get more of me so that you can feel good. You want to feel good, don't you?

Damn straight.

Okay then, go and get that money.

Next thing you knew, I was buying crack with my rent money. This maddening cycle would repeat itself every payday. It got to the point where I started buying money orders for the rent as soon as I got paid to deter me from buying crack with it. My crack dealer doesn't take money orders. After buying the amount of crack I budgeted for, I'd be back in the same predicament hours later.

Man, I need another hit right now.

Russell.

What Crack?

You can actually get a whole lot of hits, but you have to spend your rent money.

I can't. I got money orders. I already tried to use a money order to buy some of you before. The guy wouldn't take it.

Go back to where you bought the money order and cash it in. Duh!

You know something? You're right.

I always am. Let's go.

I had good intentions, but the addiction had its own agenda.

Moving Sale, But I'm Not Moving

A crack high is cheap, but all those "cheaps" add up. You spend $10 or $20 dollars and smoke it up in a few minutes. If you spend $50 on a bigger rock, you may get a better hit and smoke it longer, but it will be gone in a half hour. You go back and buy more, and that's when you realize it's your fifth time going back and all of your pockets, checking accounts, and savings accounts are all empty.

When you're out of money, what do you do? You start selling stuff. Man, I sold everything: furniture, clothes, jewelry, and anything else I owned that I could sell or barter to get more crack.

You start off taking music CDs, DVDs, and little things like that to the dealer in exchange for crack. If they didn't want it, there were people standing around who did. I'd hand the money right to the dealer and off I went. When the small things were gone, it was time to sell any watches, rings, and jewelry I had. The dealers didn't mind taking good jewelry, and they gave us less crack than cash would've bought, but who cares, I had some crack.

I emptied everything out of my apartment: the TV, toaster, blender, CD player, tools, and anything else the block or to the pawn shop would take. It was a moving sale without the moving. One time I went out at night to get some crack for Kathy and me. The next morning she says to me,

"Russell, somebody broke into our place!" she panicked.

I jumped up. "Really? When? What did they take?"

"It must have happened last night. The microwave is gone."

"Baby, you and me smoked the microwave last night."

"We did?" she asked, surprised.

"Yeah. How do you think I scored? We ain't got no money right now."

It sounded bad saying it that morning, but the night before it felt good.

I remember I hit the block to sell something. Everybody out there was looking at me funny.

"Hey, man. How much can I get for this?"

"A nightstand?" he frowned. "Don't nobody want a nightstand."

"I just brought it out here so you can see the quality of it. I'm selling the whole bedroom set."

And just like that, my bedroom set was gone. We smoked some serious 'Sealy Posturepedic' crack that night.

There was no worse feeling than taking something to the block and not getting anything for it. You feel like you belong on the short yellow bus carrying around some random object that no one wants. That really makes you look like a crackhead, yet and still, you have no crack. And no matter what you're selling, you change your sales pitch a hundred times until you sell it. If all else fails, you take it around the corner hoping someone there would at least give you $10 or $20 for it.

"Can I get an 8 ball for these," I'd ask as I showed the dealer my bargain.

"Man, get the hell outta here with those old-ass grandpa shoes."

"What? Man, these are expensive shoes. They cost me $300."

"Those things are played out. I wouldn't give you an 8 ball for those. They ain't worth $50."

"How about $40?"

"No."

"$30?"

"No."

"$15?"

"Didn't you hear me say no?"

"How about $1.36 Cut a brother a break."

"Ain't nobody got thirty-six cents out here."

You lose all your bargaining leverage on crack. Man, I ended up taking those shoes back home. There would be no oxford leather wingtips crack, for me and Kathy tonight.

They're Coming to Get Us!!

Besides making you try to sell your mamma and grandmamma for a dollar *or* a Hot Pocket, crack also plays terrible tricks on your mind. It makes you paranoid. You become suspicious of everything around you -- and everything not around you. Kathy and I always got high in our bedroom. I'd bring crack home, we'd get the pipe and the lighter, and head back there. One night we smoked a couple of good rocks. Suddenly, Kathy jumped up with her eyes wide.

"Shhhh," she said to me.

"What?"

"Be quiet."

"Why?"

"I said, 'Shhhh.'"

I shut up and watched her.

"Did you hear that?" she asked.

"Hear what?"

"That."

I listened for a few seconds. "Yeah, I hear it." I ran to the window and peeked through the blinds.

"You see them, Russell?"

"Shhhh," I told her. I was so serious. I looked around, but they were hiding. "They're coming to get us."

"Who's us?" she said fearfully.

"I don't know, but they're about to get it." I got mad. I said, "Us! Or whatever your name is, they're coming to get you! "Who down there?!" I yelled through a closed window. "Whoever's out there better show themselves instead of hiding!… "Kunta Kinte, is that you? Kissy? James from *Good Times*? Show yourself and stop hiding!"

That damn parking lot was empty as hell! I was three stories up thinking someone was looking in my window. Crack ain't right!

Who Cares About Nanny?

Somehow during Kathy and I's crack-apalooza adventures, we managed to have a beautiful, healthy daughter named Rita. There was this woman in my sister's building named Nanny that watched my sister Renee's kids. She said she'd watch Rita, so I hired her. I took my daughter over there the following Monday.

"Good morning," she said cheerfully as she opened the door.

"Good morning, Nanny."

She looked down at Rita. "Oh, she's such a pretty little girl!" She picked my daughter up and took her inside.

I brought in my daughter's bag and placed it on the couch. When she took my daughter to the back, I looked over and saw Nanny's pocketbook, with money sticking out a little bit. I snatched the money in two seconds flat.

"I'll see you later!" I yelled as I exited the door.

When I came back to pick Rita up, Kathy's sister was waiting on me with a baseball bat. She started bashing my truck – WHAM! WHAM!

"Hey!" I yelled out the window. "

"I'm going to kill you! You stole Nanny's money!"

I heard that and pulled off with the quickness. Kathy was at work and called me.

"Russell, what happened?"

I was mad that they told Kathy. "What do you mean?"

"Nanny called me and said, 'Kathy, I think your boyfriend stole my money out my purse because he was the only one in here. Did you take it?"

"Yeah, I took it." I wasn't going to lie to Kathy.

When Kathy got home, she laid into me. "Don't you ever do anything like that! That was our childcare provider! She had our baby! She could have done something to our child as payback for what you did!"

I had a mangled truck, a mad girlfriend, her enraged sister, and one pissed Nanny who felt violated by my thievery. I not only had to pay the money back, I had to find a way to get more crack that day. Damn you crack. Damn you!

CHAPTER 12

Everything Must Go!

As an electrician, I networked with a lot of carpenters, roofers, and plumbers, and we'd bring each other extra business. One plumber introduced me to his brother nicknamed, Cockeyed Junior. They named him after Cockeyed Junior, a character on a Richard Pryor record. Now Cockeyed Junior was always getting into something and he had balls of steel. We hit it off and began stealing together. I worked with some bold people before, but Cockeyed Junior was the cock of the walk. He came over one night around 9:00 pm with a stolen pickup truck.

"Man, I got this score we can do."

"What do you want me to do?"

"Just come with me."

I hopped in and went for a ride. We pulled up to an electronics store. The entire block was deathly silent.

"What are we doing?" I asked him.

"Just watch out for the po-po or security guards."

So I'm watching out and I hear a loud boom. The sound of glass shattering cut through the atmosphere.

"Russell, let's move! We're taking all these VCRs."

I ran through the glass and began grabbing boxes. We loaded the truck up with all the VCRs and took off. We went back to our neighborhood, opened the back of the truck and started selling them to our 'customers.' I set two VCRs to the side for Kathy and me, then went to work. "VCRs for only $100!" Cockeyed Junior yelled to the right side of the truck. I backed him up on the left side. "Brand new! Still in the box! $100!" They sold like hot cakes. We had 86 of them, and they sold out in three hours. We split the money and he left with the truck. I bought some crack and went home to Kathy.

I walked in with the VCRs and crack and Kathy and I got high. When we ran out, I went back and bought some more with the VCR money. Then I went back a second and a third time. After we smoked all of the VCR money, I took the VCRs I brought home and sold them for $200 – which meant $200 of crack. That's too bad. I never got to watch my "Jungle Fever" video. Oh well, maybe next time.

The Big Crack-owsky

Cockeyed Junior came and blew his horn. It's time to get money. I ran downstairs.

"You got a job for us?" I asked.

"No. I was hoping you had something."

I said, "We can go out to Virginia. We can find some good stuff to steal out there."

Some of the company trucks had their name on the side so you would know what they had inside. Electric trucks, plumbing trucks, and appliance trucks always had good stuff inside them that you could sell very quickly. If it had equipment inside that sold retail for $6,000 apiece, we'd sell it for $200 or $300. People didn't hesitate to buy expensive items. They just forked over the money.

That night, we stole some small items, but I went back out after he dropped me off. I looked around and decided to steal a huge trencher – a piece of construction equipment used to dig trenches, especially for laying pipes, cables or installing drainage. I hooked it up to my truck and drove off with it. I went to a guy that did construction work and knocked on his door.

"What's going on, Russell? It's late."

"I know. I wouldn't disturb you if I didn't have something good for you." I stepped to the side and looked back.

He looked where I was looking and his demeanor changed. "I can use something like that. I'll give you $2,000 for it."

He went in his house and came back 5 minutes later and gave me $2,000. This trencher costs $50,000, so he got over big. It didn't cost me nothing, but some gas. That was one of my biggest heists – and it was the biggest for a single item. I took a nice amount of that money straight to the dealer, but first I had to take care of my lady. Before scoring, I stopped at the liquor store.

That night was all about romance. I turned off the lights, poured both of us a glass of red wine, and we smoked crack and got high by candlelight. Now only if we had one of those VCRs I stole, that would've made the night perfect.

Free High is the Worst High

Free high is when someone comes over with crack, lets you smoke a little bit of it, you get paranoid, and then they leave you without enough to get high some more. It's like crack magically appears, gets you all hot and bothered, then leaves you with your draws at your ashy knees. Man, that makes a crackhead angrier than a toothless Pitbull eating meat.

Many times, I'd want another hit so bad, I'd literally get on my hands and knees and search the floor to find crack crumbs. Any white or light beige substance I saw would make me grab it and inspect it. I grabbed pieces of dirt, paper, bread crumbs, lint. That was all free high's fault. We used to have people over our house every day after 5pm to smoke, and sometimes the person we knew would bring someone with them. Kathy went out with her girlfriend Jerri and Jerri met some dude that was all up in her face and looked like he had a few dollars.

He took Jerri out the next night and she came to our place all excited afterwards talking about, "Girl, he spent a whole bunch of money! We smoked all day!"

Kathy said, "What?! For real?"

"Mmm-hmmm. He even gave me some to take home," she said proudly.

She pulled out a dirty and burned up pipe. We cleaned the pipe of the rez, put the rez to the side for us to smoke when Jerri left, then smoked the rocks she brought over.

I hadn't seen the dude yet, but when she came over a few days later, the guy came with her. He had a lot of crack. I knew the dude from high school, so we had a lot of fun catching up while firing up the pipe. Since me and the dude knew each other, it messed up he and Jerri's connection because the dude started coming over after that day without her. And he always brought crack with him. That's another lesson about free high – if you take someone that buys you crack to one of your friend's house and they hit it off with your friend, be prepared to get cheated on. There's no loyalty in the crack game.

One of the worst offenders of free high was my youngest brother, Wayne. And Kathy and I were his unsuspecting victims. I remember he popped up at our place with crack.

"What's up?" he asked.

"What's up?" I shot back anxiously. "You scored?"

"Yep."

He opened his hand and showed me a big boulder rock. That thing looked like a diamond that belonged in a museum behind a case with armed guards watching over it! He sat down at the table. I sat across from him and Kathy sat next to me. He put that huge rock in the pipe, lit it, and it took him away. He slowly placed the pipe on the table and pushed it away. That was our chance! I reached for the pipe, and he looked at me violently and snatched it back.

"Man, backup! Backup!" He sat up really fast, and looked around, paranoid.

Kathy and I wanted that pipe so bad, but he was being stingy. All we could do was wait for him. He never took another hit. He just picked up the pipe, looked at us, put it in his pocket, and broke out. I was mad as hell at him. The crack was right there in front of us! I could hear it sizzling when he fired it up. The pipe was in my hand for a second, but I never got to smoke it!

My brother would drop in all the time and pull that free-high bull on us. But after that time, he always let us get a hit or two before leaving us wanting more. This happened over and over again, and we were defenseless to it. Like I said before, free high is the worst high.

Interception

Crack will make you selfish. If the addiction is kicking in really badly, all you'll think about is your own high. Everyone else doesn't matter. I don't care if it was your mother, father, business partner, best friend, cousin, brother, sister, wife, or even God.

I was craving a hit so badly one evening that I scored and didn't tell Kathy. I came home with rocks in my pocket and kept it to myself.

Don't tell her about me, the crack said, *because you know she's going to smoke half of me. Keep me all to yourself.*

That's a good idea, I replied.

Kathy was on her own.

I walked through the door, and there she was.

"Hey, baby," I said as I kissed her and walked away.

"How was your day?" she asked.

"Fine," I said as I reached the hallway.

"Did you score?"

"No," I said as I reached the bathroom.

I didn't smoke any of it. There was a canister on a shelf way above the toilet, and I hid the crack in there. It was so high that I had to stand on the toilet seat to put them up there. The plan was to smoke up my new late-night stash when Kathy was fast asleep.

We ended up having company that night, and when they left, I was ready to get high. My whole attitude changed because all I wanted to do was be alone with my crack. I was going to get high as the sun and I wasn't going to have to share it with anybody. Once they left, I hurried to the bathroom. I stood on that toilet, got the canister down, opened it… and it was empty! I went into the bedroom and there was Kathy enjoying the high I was supposed to be enjoying. "Want some, with your selfish ass?" she said. I smiled at her and said, "You damn crackhead."

CHAPTER THIRTEEN

Bad, Worse, Worst

I was outside minding my own business waiting for my brother Larry. That's when a dude came up to me.

"Yo, where is Southern Avenue?"

"Well, you go down there—"

"*Whop!*"

Before I could finish my statement, the dude hauled off and punched me in my face! That joker hit me hard, too. Maybe I did something to somebody he knew, or it was a gang initiation – I don't know. Whatever the reason, I wasn't going to bother asking why. He ran one way, and I ran the other way back to the apartment.

"Kathy! This dude just hit me in my mouth!"

She looked at my jaw and put some ice on it, but the pain wouldn't go away. That's when Kevin came over.

"Russell, I know where to get the good stuff."

"Oh yeah? Where?"

"They got some nice working 50s, too."

"I have $100. Let's go."

I knew some crack would make my jaw feel better. I made Kevin stop at the liquor store so I could get some beer to take away the pain until we could score. I drank two Red Bull malt liquors within 5 minutes and I couldn't feel my jaw hurting anymore. I was feeling good.

We went into DC, and I got out to score.

"How much you want to buy?" one guy asked.

Another guy stepped up. "I'm serving him," he told everyone else. "How much you want?"

Some dealers try to enforce the rule that whatever dealer sees you first, you have to buy from him from now on. Well, I saw a guy I knew from jail, so I looked past the two dudes that approached me and pointed to the person I knew from jail.

"I ain't talking to you two. I want to see that man right there," I pointed.

"Oh, you're not buying from us?" the first dude asked.

I don't remember much else. They beat me so bad, my whole jaw was swollen. I was so dazed and messed up that I don't know how I found my way back to Kevin's car. When I got there, the police came out of nowhere.

"Put your hands in the air!"

"What did I do?" I asked.

"You look like a robbery suspect!"

"That wasn't me! I just came up the street!"

They checked me out and let me go. When we got home, I realized my money was gone. They robbed me, beat me up, and took my money.

"You ain't going to believe this," I said to Kathy. "I got jumped by ten dudes. Every time one got tired of whooping me, another one took over and whooped me like he was my daddy!

Kathy was scared because my whole face was swollen. I was really furious because I ain't have no money, no crack, my face looked like a blowfish, and guess who shows up? My brother Wayne... with minuscule crumbs of crack rock we called, 'kibbles and bits.'

"Wayne," I said, trying to get some sympathy so that he'd give me more crack. "Look at my face."

"Daaaaaaaamn!" he said. "Alright, I got something. I got something." He pulled out a crack rock and broke me and Kathy off a piece so small, we needed a magnifying glass to see it.

I said, "Man, if you don't get that tiny pebble out of here! What do I look like, an ant?" He proceeded to break me off a slightly bigger piece. When I finished smoking that pea-sized rock, I settled in for a nice ride on the Crack Shuttle. I looked over at Wayne and he was staring at me with a quizzical gaze.

"What?" I said. "Can you loan me some money. I'm hungry." I dug in my pocket and gave him a crinkled dollar bill. He scowled at me and said, "What am I supposed to get with this?" Kathy said, "Some kibbles and bits." We laughed so hard, it almost ruined our high.

Crack Daddies

People have a misconception about crackheads. The stereotypes always have them being between the ages of 20 and 50, but crack doesn't discriminate. Crack is an equal opportunity addiction, and old people can get caught up, too.

I went to a crack house and there was an 80-year-old man in there. 80! Man, this dude had white hair, his eyes were yellowish, and his arching shoulders gave him a slight humpback. He had a slow elderly walk and wore thick, Poindexter glasses. The man was plain old sitting there with a crack pipe in his hand.

I looked at the dude next to me. "What is that old man doing in here?"

He pointed to a young, sexy girl walking into the room from the kitchen.

"Oh, that's why he's here," I nodded my head.

The vixen sashayed over to the Old Man, placed her hand on his thigh, and whispered something flirty in his ear. He went into his pocket and gave her $100. She left and came back with some crack, and then she helped him hold the pipe to his face. He took a hit and got higher than the Space Shuttle in orbit. He closed his eyes, sat back, and his chest began heaving so heavily that it looked like it was about to jump through his Bill Cosby sweater.

I said, "This man is about to have a heart attack over here."

No one did anything, especially the young girl. As his old body went through the trauma of getting high, the young girl was smoking up his crack. He was getting tricked out of his money by a young girl.

"I'm getting the heck up out of here. If this man dies, we're all going to jail." I quickly left out of there and didn't look back. I went to get some crack from somebody else because I didn't want any part of this scene.

A lot of young girls get on crack. They prey on old men who want to be in their company and then trick them into being their crack daddies. Now, the girls are getting free highs off the poor, helpless old dudes. And when his money is gone, the girl moves on to the next old man she can trick, and all that's left is an old, elderly, strung out crackhead. Sad.

CHAPTER FOURTEEN

Three Ain't A Charm

I came across a new townhouse development during construction. It was a very busy jobsite. I parked my truck and acted like I was one of the contractors. I rolled my dolly into one of the houses and came out with a refrigerator. That's when a guy walked up on me.

"What are you doing?" he asked.

I was always quick on my feet. "Man, a guy told me to come to this lot and pick this refrigerator up. Can you help me load it into the truck?"

"Yeah," he said.

He had no idea he was helping a stranger steal from his employer! We loaded it up; I took it away, and sold it. The next day, I went back and stole a truck full of refrigerators and stoves. Doing these heists gave me a rush only surpassed by crack. But just like my crack high, the rush would fade quickly. It was just getting good, when I went back the third time, but the site was now being monitored by a security guard. Apparently, somebody was stealing refrigerators and stoves and they couldn't figure out how. Aww, such a shame. The rookie security guard was eyeing his clipboard as he stood in front of my truck.

"Can I see in the back of your truck?" he asked with suspicion.

"For what?"

"Because somebody's been stealing from our job site."

"It ain't me."

"Well, I need to look in the back of your truck."

I wasn't about to open my truck and show him all the stuff I just stole. "You ain't looking in the back of my truck."

He was coming toward me, so I hit the gas and popped the clutch. I almost hit that rascal, but he moved out the way just in time. Unfortunately for me, he wrote my tag number down and reported it to the police.

My truck was registered in my father's name, so the police went to my parents' house. The police looked around the house and in the backyard looking for stolen refrigerators and stoves. What's funny is I sold my father a stolen refrigerator, but it wasn't marked where anyone could identify it – and it had been there for six months, so it was used and broken in and not seen as new.

All those police on my parents' property damn near gave my grandmother a heart attack. Since the police were on my trail, I couldn't go back there. So, I found a nice four-star crack house with all of the amenities and laid low.

The cops eventually found me because somebody reported seeing the truck at the crime scene and reported the license plate. They asked me about my involvement.

"Somebody stole my truck," I said with an honest look.

"Did you report it?"

"For what? It was gone and I didn't know who took it."

Thank goodness they didn't take me back for the security guy to identify!

Appliances R Us

I had the process of stealing from model homes and new developments down to a science. I would steal from the model home at night, and if the setup was sweet enough and there were enough new homes around, I'd leave a development with my truck full of refrigerators and stoves. It was great money because I wasn't working on the job as an electrician anymore. Everything I did as an electrician was on the side, so this model-home hustle was what put crack on the table.

I was driving around looking for new developments and saw a small appliance store. I saw an opportunity, so I parked my truck and went inside.

"I'd like to speak with the owner, please."

"I'm the owner," the man said.

"Look here, I have these refrigerators. Are you looking to buy any?"

"How many do you have?"

"I'll give you as many as you want? I have some stoves, too."

He was all about that money because he didn't ask me where I got them from. All he wanted was the appliances at bargain prices and that's what I gave him. He bought every refrigerator and stove I brought to him. And I went back over and over again. He was making a killing due to his new appliance wholesaler and I was making thousands of dollars.

Everything was running smoothly until I gave my cousin a few dollars to help me unload my truck after a serious heist. Big mistake that was! I didn't know he was hanging around me waiting for his chance to come up on some money. So, when I messed around and got high that night, he took my keys and stole my truck! He went and stole some appliances of his own, took them to the appliance shop I was working with, and tried to sell them to the owner like I did. The owner wouldn't buy any from him, so this fool robbed the owner, took his wallet, brought my truck back, and put the keys in my apartment.

I went out the next morning and noticed my car was parked in a different parking space. I got inside it to go do a hustle and found a wallet. When I opened it, I almost passed out. Inside the wallet was a police badge and identification – the appliance store owner was a cop! I took his wallet back and found out what happened. The owner/policeman didn't believe I wasn't in on the robbery, so he wouldn't do business with me anymore. That was my main selling connection, and my cousin destroyed it. Damn.

Kathy's cousin learned what I was doing and tried to do it, too. She went out and stole some refrigerators, but the police came after her. Instead of pulling over, she tried to flee and crashed the truck into a pole at over 100 mph. She died on the scene trying to do my hustle. You had to be smart and patient to do what I was doing. You would think the tragedy of losing my business connection because of my cousin robbing the owner and Kathy's cousin dying in a horrific car crash would've slowed me down a bit, but it didn't. Not one bit.

Binky and the Rez

Sometimes we didn't use a crack pipe to get high. Whenever we broke ours and buying a new one was too expensive, we made 'binkies.' A binky is a makeshift pipe made from a sample liquor bottle and an aspirin bottle. You put a hole in the side of the aspirin bottle, put a hole in the bottom of the liquor bottle, then place the bottle in the side of the aspirin bottle. The liquor bottle serves as your mouthpiece and you tie a rubber band around it to keep it in place. Next, you put aluminum foil over the top of the aspirin bottle and put cigarette ashes in it. The ashes stop the coke from draining too fast when you're smoking. The last step is to poke some holes in the foil and that's it. You have a binky, and they were perfect to smoke with.

The heat melts the crack and crystalizes it. The crystals would stick on the side of the pipe or the foil, and all the good residue would fall in the inside. At the end of the night when we had no more crack left, we'd take the pipe, put some alcohol in it, shake it up real good, and pour it on top of a mirror. Then we'd light it with a match, and it would burn and burn, until it eventually burned out. Then we'd let it dry, scrape it all up with a razor blade, and we'd have what we called the *rez*, which is short for residue. We'd put the rez into the pipe and smoke all over again.

Smoking residue is better than the rocks it came from, and people used to fight over it. It was serious business regarding who got the rez. They'd go Captain Kirk over the rez. As soon as the rock disintegrated, someone would yell, "I want the rez! I want the rez!"

Sometimes we'd let rez build up in a pipe for a couple of months until it built up so much that you couldn't smoke crack out of it anymore. See, the flame kills everything inside of the crack rock, so the rez will be pure coke for the most part. All the cut, baking soda, and water are gone, so what you get from the rez is a really big rush. You know the saying, "the blacker the berry, the sweeter the juice?" The same goes for rez... The blacker the rez, the sweeter the high.

Cut The Damn Lights Off!

After the birth of our son, Kathy's friend, Jerri, started hanging out at our place all the time. She was really cool, but her boyfriend was in jail and she kept accepting his collect calls from *our phone*! The next thing we knew, our phone bill was higher than our yearly allotment for crack. Needless to say, the phone got cut off. Then our neighbors moved in with their boy and girl. Now our kids could have somebody to play with. We'd let them play together in the front room while we all would go in the back room and get high. Every now and then, Kathy would go out front and check on the kids.

Our new roommates got comfortable. Not only weren't they helping pay any bills, they were smoking our crack. Instead of Kathy and me splitting everything, we had to divide our crack four ways. They were getting a free high on my dime, and I didn't like that. Furthermore, nothing we did could get them to leave. They were like cockroaches.

But when the cable, phone and electricity got cut off, I learned some very useful information – if you want to get rid of some crackheads, get your electricity cut off. Our freeloading roommates left the same day the electricity got cut off. Crackheads hate not having electricity.

Since I'm an electrician, you know exactly what I did – I went downstairs and cut everything back on, but I waited until the freeloading roommates left. The good part was that Kathy and I had all our crack to ourselves. (singing) "We're in heaven."

Two months later, the electric company sent a letter stating they were going to find who tampered with the electricity and press charges. All roads pointed to me, so we borrowed money from Kathy's father and paid the bill. Want to get rid of a crackhead? Get your electricity cut off.

CHAPTER FIFTEEN

Where Hath My Crack Dealer Gone?

Kathy had her experiences with free high. She was ironing her clothes and getting ready for work when her friend Sherry came over at 7:30 in the morning. Kathy let her in.

"Hey, girl, what are you doing over here so early? Is everything okay?"

"What are you doing?" her friend asked as if she hadn't heard the questions Kathy asked her.

"I'm about to go to work."

"You want to take a hit?"

"Okay, I got a few minutes."

Sherry pulled out a binky and they went to the dining room table. She put the crack on the binky and went to work on smoking it. Kathy took a puff. Sherry took a couple more puffs and gave it back to Kathy. After one more puff, she took it back and smoked the rest of it up. Sherry was feeling nice as she got up.

"Damn, that was good," she said with wide eyes. "I'll be right back."

"Where are you going?" asked Kathy.

"To buy some more."

When I came home on my lunch break, Kathy was standing at the window.

"Is everything okay?" I asked her.

"Yes. I'm just waiting for Sherry."

"I didn't know you were off today."

"I'm not. Did you see Sherry out there?"

"No. Did you call your job to tell them you weren't coming in?"

"I'm still going in. I'm just waiting for Sherry. I'm going in after she gets here."

I went back to work and when I came home at the end of the day, Kathy was still looking out the window for Sherry. That free high had her geekin'. As I was heading to bed for a night cap, I looked out into the dining room and saw Kathy still standing at the window waiting for Sherry to come back. Crack is a monster.

Trick the Police

On New Year's Eve night, I was in a pickup truck. Kathy was home 6-months pregnant and I just scored. That crack had me speeding home to get to that pipe to smoke it. I was happy as a lucky pick-6 lottery winner until the flashing blue and red sirens came up behind me.

"Oh my god!" I yelled as I pulled to the side. "I'm going to jail!" I was speeding with a pocket full of crack. I know I'm a goner.

The policeman came up to my window. "Why are you in so much of a hurry?"

"Man, my wife is pregnant. I'm trying to get home to take her to the hospital."

"I don't believe you."

"Here's my cell phone." I grabbed it and began dialing. "I'll let you talk to my wife."

"No, that's okay," he said as he waved his hand. "Go ahead, but slow down."

I couldn't believe it! I was free to go! I had talked myself out of another jam. If he'd accepted that phone, I would've been in major trouble because the phone didn't work! I had a few dead cell phones in the truck, and I just grabbed one to tell my lie. When he walked away, I dialed Kathy and realized that I fell for my own trick. I couldn't wait to get through the door to tell her what happened.

"Kathy," I said when I opened the door, "you're not going to believe what I had to go through to get here."

She said, "Come on, the ball's about to drop." I sat next to her and quickly lit up a rock in the pipe. Just as the notorious ball in New York City's Time Square was falling, "4 – 3 -2 -1," we took a hit from the pipe. Happy New Year!

Hold My Truck

I never had a problem getting a job; my problem was keeping one. When I got another job as a supervisor, I bought a truck to carry my tools everywhere I went. I used the truck on my 9 to 5 and also on my side jobs. I always had a way of getting money whether legal or illegal, and the side jobs meant money would always come in no matter what was going on with my 9 to 5. Since I was doing so well there, I had lots of money from my side jobs to spend getting high.

I always came home every day with money or crack – I made a point of having one or the other. I'd make a hustle out of anything and I'd never miss a day to come up with something to bring home: $20, $30, or $40 to get high with.

Sometimes the hustles got slow or I couldn't find anything, and that's when things got tricky.

"What's up?" I said as I rolled up on one of my main dealers.

"What's up? How much you need?"

"How much can I get until payday?" I asked desperately.

"You can't get a damn thing until payday. You know I don't give credit."

"I'm good for it," I tried to persuade him.

"I'll tell you what, I'll give you a couple of 50s if you let me hold your truck."

That was a no-brainer. "Can you have it back by 5am?"

"Yeah."

"Okay," I said as I got out. "You know where I live, right? Just put the keys under my doormat."

That became a habit whenever I didn't have any money and no hustle – let them hold my truck for the night. Some of them took good care of it, some of them used it to deliver drugs out of, and some used it to smoke weed and have sex with women in the back. Then there were some that drove it all over the place. I'd get it back sometimes and say, "How in the hell he put 600 miles on my car in one night?" They probably drove to Atlantic City or New York or somewhere having fun. Crack helped me start another side business, truck rental. I gave unlimited miles as long as you had it back before I went to work at 5 am.

Fake Money, Real A$$ Whooping!

It was snowing and I was trying to figure out a way to get high. That's when Peanut and Thomas came to my home.

"Yo, Russell, let's go cop some crack," Thomas said.

I said, "I ain't got no money."

Peanut handed a folded $50 bill to me. "I have plenty of money."

I took the $50 bill and got excited because I knew we would get a jumbo for all that money! We'd get a nice high. I unfolded the bill and realized it was fake.

"Man, this is fake."

Thomas began laughing. "Yeah, but you didn't know it at first. We're going to pull a scam. We'll buy some crack with it and be gone before they realize it."

It sounded like a great idea to me. "Let's do it," I said.

We got in Kathy's car and headed through the snow down to Southern Avenue, which is the hood. We hit the hot spot and I went to score with the fake money.

One dealer stepped away from the others. "What you need?"

"A 50 rock."

"Alright."

He gave me a jumbo, and I handed him the money and got back in the car with Peanut and Thomas.

"Hey, come back here!" the dealer yelled.

Man, they must've thought I was a fool to go back there. I hit that gas and pulled off. I sped down Southern Avenue about a mile and started to relax.

"Here they come!" Peanut yelled. "They're behind us!"

I checked the mirror and just as he said, the dealer and one of his buddies were behind us. They chased me from Southern Avenue to the highway. I was dipping through traffic the best I could in the snow, but those guys wouldn't give up. They must've had those real good snow tires. I didn't think $50 would be so important to them.

I ran into a few cars and almost hit this guy walking across the street. That scared me so much, I stopped this car chase nonsense.

I asked Peanut, "How many guys are in the car?"

"Two," Thomas answered.

My mind was made up. "We're going to fight them. It's three of us and two of them. We're going to fight these dudes tonight. No more running. You ready?"

"Yeah, I'm ready," Peanut said.

I pulled the car over, and we jumped out. The dealers stopped and got out of their car. I threw up my guards and looked to my left and right, only to realize I was alone. Peanut and Thomas were halfway down the road running like track stars. Ain't that a bitch! I had to fight these rough, burly dudes by myself. One guy came at me with a razor and cut me good – straight across my face from my mouth all the way up my cheek and past my ear. Then they stabbed up my body. I had on a leather coat, but they ripped right through that. Blood seeped from everywhere as I fell to the ground. They left me for dead. When they were gone, I somehow got back in the car and headed home. It was cold as hell driving because they bust one of the windows out of the car. I made it home around 1:00 in the morning and Kathy took me to the hospital. I ended up with stitches in my mouth and face, and they patched up all of my wounds. The doctor said I lost so much blood that I should've been dead. After getting patched up, I rested at home for a little while.

Peanut and Thomas came to see me when they found out I was home.

"You alright, man?" Peanut asked.

"Yeah, I'll be fine. Man, why'd y'all run?"

"I was going to fight," Thomas said, "but I saw him reach for a weapon."

"Yeah," Peanut chimed in. "I thought he was about to shoot us."

"He didn't have a gun. It was a razor blade."

"Well," Peanut began, "I wasn't going to wait around to find out."

I know they say cocaine is a 'hell of a drug,' but crack makes you do the dumbest shit. You'll literally do anything for a hit. So, when I got back on my feet, I got some money and went back to the same hood. The same guys that almost killed me recognized me instantly. I didn't care. I was all about that crack.

"Hey, you're the guy that gave us that fake money," the one that sliced me up with the razor said.

"It wasn't me. I was with those guys, but I didn't give you the fake money. It was the other two dudes that ran. I apologize for that."

They were caught off guard and loosened up to me.

"Alright," the main dealer said as he went relaxed the tension in his face. "What do you want?"

"A 50." I handed him a real $50 bill. He checked it, then smiled, and handed me my rock and I went on my merry way.

CHAPTER SIXTEEN

Hotel Crackifornia

I suffered a broken nose while on a job, and the medical bills were racking up. The company wanted me to agree to stop going to the hospital in exchange for a lump-sum settlement. I saw all those zeros on the check and knew it was party time. I was thinking about buying enough crack to last a week. I was planning on calling my job and taking the whole week off. But as I got in the car with Kathy and rushed to cash the check to get some crack, we got into a bad car accident.

The car insurance company offered us huge settlements, and we accepted them. I told this woman that was selling crack about the settlement and that we needed a ride to go see the lawyer and sign the checks. I also told her I'd buy a couple hundred dollars of crack from her. So she drove us down there. It was perfect because she knew her way around downtown DC and we didn't have to pay for parking or make Kathy walk far since she was pregnant.

We got downtown and met the lawyer at a restaurant. We ate, got our checks, and left. My settlement was $5,000, and Kathy got $7,000. She got sick when we left, so we dropped her off at home. I wanted to get at least a 50 or an 8-ball of crack because we'd been getting high all night and I didn't need a whole lot.

The girl took me to a place that cashed checks without requiring I.D., and that was the only place I could get the check cashed. It was right next to a hotel. I cashed the check and got back in the car.

"You cash it?" she asked.

"Yes, indeed."

"You don't have to wait until we get back to the neighborhood. I'll give you some crack right now."

"Okay. Let me go grab a hotel room right here."

I gave her the money, got the crack, checked in, and she left. I smoked by myself and got a good paranoid high. I knew somebody was going to catch me smoking so I took the smoke detector out of the ceiling so it wouldn't go off and threw it under the bed.

I called my sister, Fuzzy, and her husband, Roach, to protect myself from being robbed. What I would do sometimes was give my sister my money and use her as a bank. When I needed more money, I'd call her to tell her to bring me more instead of having all of it on me at one time. She came over and got $3,000 from me. Then I called the dealer back.

"Hey, this is Russell. I need some more. Are you nearby?"

"I never left."

"Good. I'm in room 228. Bring it on up."

"How much?"

"Give me a couple of 8-balls."

She brought them to me and I went to work on them. I called her an hour later.

"Hey, you still here?"

"What you need?"

"A couple more 8-balls."

"I can't keep walking in and out of this hotel. They're going to think I'm up to something."

She said the right thing to make me spend more money because I was still paranoid.

"You're right. Make that *three* 8-balls because I have to go home soon."

"You only want three?"

"Bring me five."

This cycle repeated itself over and over again. In between them, there were phone calls to my sister. I got so paranoid from smoking that I called my brother.

"Wayne, come on over. I got some stuff you won't believe."

"I'm on my way."

"I'm not at home. I'm at the hotel next to the no-I.D. check cashing place downtown."

Wayne came over and got so high that he left and never came back. That's the first time Wayne never came back. He was messed up!

I called the dealer to bring me a few more 8-balls, and then I called my sister. She came through the door with sad news.

"This is it, Russell."

"What, you ain't coming back?" I asked concerned.

"No, I'm not coming back because you ain't got no more money. This is all that's left."

"Alright. Shoot!"

After I ran out, I sat there for two hours geekin'. I already smoked the rez so there was absolutely nothing left to smoke. I called my sister again.

"Look, the dealer left, so y'all gotta come get me. I ain't got no more crack and I'm out of money."

Roach went and picked up Kathy and they came and got me. Kathy was ready to go upside my head when she saw me. I went home looking like a rag doll. I had the same clothes on that I was wearing the day before. I ain't showered. I ain't do nothing but sit there and get high.

"I'm sorry for not coming home last night," I said to Kathy.

"Last night? What about the other nights?"

"What other nights?"

"Russell, you've been gone for five days."

"Five days!"

I couldn't believe it. I'd been in that room for five days making love to that crack pipe! I was out of my settlement money, so I became fixated on getting my hands on Kathy's settlement money so I could continue the festivities. I swiped her bankcard and withdrew money from the cash machine every chance I could get. I didn't get all of it, but I damn sure smoked a few thousand dollars of it. And this time I didn't rent a room and binge for five days. Nope, I smoked it in the comfort of our home.

A Crack Convention

I'm a people person and I'm very nice to people. I make friends easily because I can talk to anybody. I knew so many people that like to get high that I began allowing them to come in our apartment. I once only allowed them to come over after 5pm, but when I lost my regular job, they began coming over all day long. It was quiet there when we moved in, but now our party was going 24 hours a day. It was like a crack convention.

Jason, our neighbor on the floor, hated us being there because our nonstop crackhead traffic interfered with his weed business. He always locked the main entrance of the building at a certain time of the night to protect himself from being robbed, but we kept opening the door and also propping it open for our friends. When we were too busy to come open the door, they'd bang on the door until someone from one of the other apartments opened it or they'd throw rocks at our windows to get our attention. It made Jason paranoid because it was drawing attention to his weed business. When we used to get high, he'd keep going in and out of his apartment to disturb us because he knew noise made crackheads paranoid. Finally, he bought a mobile home and parked it out front so the weed heads didn't have to come into the apartment with the crack people.

I could talk a zebra out his stripes. If you came to my house, I was going to get some crack from you one way or another. Either you were going to give it to me or I was going to take it – simple as that. Especially the cheap people! They'd come in your house all night long and kibble and bit you to death. I put up with it just waiting for a chance to get more out of them. If they put the pipe down, dropped a rock or a crumb, or even turned their head for too long, I'd get 'em!

Kathy and I took turns getting high. One would go get high in the back room, and the other person would watch the kids. I'd always put something to the side for her.

You'd be surprised who's a crackhead. People of all age groups and professions would come over and smoke all night long. Some people would smoke until the sun came up because that told them it was time to get to work. A deacon used to come over, smoke all night, and before he left in the morning, he'd pray. I stood there with him and prayed he would come back that night with more crack. My prayers were often answered. Hallelujah!

Mo' Babies, Mo' Problems

I was supposed to go to court over a traffic violation, but I never showed up. Kathy was pregnant and I had to keep making money to get high and keep things moving. Kathy knew that dust was bad for the baby, so she knew not to smoke that. But no one knew back then that crack could be hazardous to your baby's health, so she kept smoking it. One thing for sure was I wasn't going to pay traffic tickets as long as I was addicted. Buying crack was much more important than sending money to the city.

I had a guy take me to court, and while heading there it began snowing so bad that traffic backed up. I finally got there an hour late.

"What's your name?" the judge asked.

"Russell Thornton."

"Mr. Thornton, do you have $150 to pay your violations?"

"No, Your Honor."

"Lock him up!" he yelled to the bailiff.

They put a bench warrant out for me on the spot because I was late. When I got there late they locked me up on the spot.

Kathy was pregnant and I wouldn't dare try to get her to come get me in all that snow. I knew my father wasn't going to get me out, but I called him anyway just so he could tell everyone I was locked up. To my surprise, my father came up there in all that snow and got me out. I knew it was nothing but the Lord working on my father. I could not believe it. I was amazed he did that for me. It turns out, the only reason he came up there to get me is because Kathy was pregnant. He was looking out for her, not me. That sounds about right.

Our daughter, Rita, was having trouble breathing around that time. Even though we were high, we knew something was wrong. It turns out she had bronchial asthma. Upon learning that, Kathy and I vowed not to smoke around her anymore. Kathy sat in the hospital for three days with her because she was so little. When they released her, we stopped letting people come over and smoke in the house anymore. The party life slowed down considerably.

When our son, Rock, was born, Kathy spent the night with him, too, until he was released. Since we weren't married, the hospital didn't allow me to stay the night with them. I walked five miles to the hospital and back every day just to see them. I was high, but I wanted to see and be with my family.

What Am I Buying?

One thing you can't do when buying crack is thoroughly look at the product before you buy it. You don't have time because you're in a hot zone. You have to be street smart out on the avenue. You don't have time. That's how people get beat.

There's a 50-50 chance you'll get something fake every time you buy something from someone new. They'll sell you peanuts or something and rush the transaction. You look at it for a couple of seconds and keep it moving. Never buy from someone off to the side by themselves and away from other dealers. Those are the ones that will beat you. Those type of people usually stand alone because dealers don't want to be around them because they're subject to get killed for taking advantage of people. Sometimes the fakers would let you taste it to make sure it's real, but then they started putting Orajel and stuff on peanuts so when you tasted it, your tongue would get numb and you'd think you got the real deal.

One time I bought $400 worth of fake crack. I was ready to get high and got back to the hotel only to find out it was soap. They were making money beating me, so we started doing the same thing. We got good at it. We broke down some macadamia nuts, put them in bags, hit the strip, got our money, and was ghost. A crackhead will do anything to get money. Sometimes people will switch up the bags. They'll show the customer the real thing when they agree to buy it, then they'll use sleight of hand and give them something different in an identical bag. As hard as crackheads work and scheme to get money, it breaks their hearts when they lose it all on fake crack. What if a crackhead was scoring for a group of friends? He'd get back with no crack, and they'd think he stole the money so he could smoke without them later. There is no honor among crackheads. Zilch. Zero.

And scoring was an even bigger risk than getting beat out of your money. We got robbed at gunpoint a few times trying to score crack. Did it stop us from going back out there to buy some more? Hell naw! As long as we could get crack, we went back again and again.

Kathy was hanging out front with her girlfriend and a dude named Stan. They walked away from Kathy and went across the street to score, but they got robbed for their money. The dude she was with got shot and killed. When that gun went off, Kathy came running up the stairs like a hurdler and came into the house with fear all over her face. Her pants were wet because she peed on herself.

"We got robbed!" she screamed. "They killed Stan!"

I went to the window and there was Stan lying across the street, dead. He was a good dude.

CHAPTER SEVENTEEN

You Better Not Sleep

Whenever smokers came over, you wanted to hide your crack from them because you didn't want them to know you had any crack. If they didn't think you had any, they'd give you more of theirs. If they knew you had some, they'd give you crumbs and try to smoke yours when theirs was gone.

One day we were sitting in the house with this dude. He was sitting in our chair, but he was so tired. I mean, he was totally drained.

He said, "Man, I have to find somewhere to sleep."

You know me. I said, "You're right there in the chair. Just go to sleep. But first, let's get high real quick."

"No, when I wake up we'll get high."

I was desperate. He was sitting there asleep and the wheels in my head were turning. I pulled Kathy into the backroom.

"Kathy, we're going to get 'em." I went in there and lightly touched his pocket. He ain't move. I reached in his pocket, grabbed a bag, and pulled it out. He was still sleeping.

"Get another one," Kathy whispered.

I got another one, and then we went in the backroom and got high as Cootie Brown! Dude woke up hours later, and we were in there waiting for him.

"Man, I feel good!" he said and stretched his arms in the air. "Okay, let's get high." He went in his pocket felt around. "Damn! Somebody stole it!"

"Stole what?" I asked.

"All my crack!" He kept feeling around in his pockets, but he didn't know that crack was gone forever.

I said, "It must have been that girl that came up in here. She was talking to you, and the next thing I knew, she was gone. She must have got you for your crack."

"Huh?" he asked in total confusion.

"Yeah, she got you. She was rubbing all over you and sweet talking you. You were talking back, so I assumed you liked it. Me and Kathy left the room to give y'all some privacy."

"How did she look? Was she fine?"

"Man, she was *real* fine."

He got up and left out the apartment patting his pockets with every step.

Kathy and I laughed when the door closed. We got him real good!

I Ain't Afraid Of No Stinking Gun!

I went to cop some crack for me and Kathy, but this particular time, I wasn't trying to buy a $10 or $20 rock – I had *$250*. I walked all the way up to the strip on Eastern Avenue.

There were two dudes out there with trench coats in 70-degree weather. That should've been a red flag, but that day, it wasn't. And these dudes weren't who I usually copped from, but my addiction made me blind to my street senses. I walked right over to them.

"How much you need?" the first guy asked.

"$250 worth."

"Come on and follow me," he said and led me away.

We got around the corner of the building, and he pulled a gun out on me.

"Whoa!" I said as I threw my hands up. "You robbing me?"

"Yeah," he confirmed with gritted teeth. "Give me all your money."

"All I have is $50."

"Naw, you told me you had $250."

"You misunderstood me. I only have $50."

"Well, give me that."

"I'm not giving you my $50," I protested.

"Give it up or I'mma shoot your ass!"

"But if I give my $50 to you, how am I going to buy some crack?"

He aimed his gun at me and pulled the trigger. It misfired.

"Come on!" his partner panicked. "The police are coming!"

They ran one way; I ran the other way… down the street to buy some crack from someone else. I was not going home without $250 worth of crack. You better recognize.

WIC Way Is Up?

My buddy Duane and I used to work for WIC, and the guy in-charge was in the parking lot next to his fancy car with a sad look on his face.

"What's going on?" I asked him. "Is something wrong?"

"Look," he said as he pointed down. "My tire is flat."

"That ain't nothing," Duane said. "You want me to fix it?"

"Fixing it isn't the problem. That tire is rare and expensive. I can't put a different tire on it because it will mess up the traction."

"We can get you that same tire in a couple hours," I told him. I didn't know where I could get the tire, but if there was some money to be made on a task, I'd find a way to get it done.

His face lit up like a Christmas tree. He looked at me with raised brows. "If you get me this same tire, I'll give you $400."

He wasn't even finished his sentence before Duane and I were walking to our truck. We rode up and down the streets looking for those tires and we found a car that had them. He parked and kept lookout while I quickly unscrewed the lug nuts. Then I started jacking up the car, but I only had to take it about three inches off the ground before the tire shifted. Duane pulled it off and threw it in the truck, while I grabbed the jack – time elapsed: 90 seconds. Damn, we were good!

We took the rim and the tire back to him, and he gave us $200 apiece. Then we got to work and made our deliveries like any other day.

From that day forward, he gave us lots of WIC items off the books such as cheese, cereal, and eggs, which meant we could use it or sell it and keep the money. We'd sell the stuff to little Mom & Pop grocery stores and make $100 or $200 apiece. I took some home for the family, which meant, you guessed it, I didn't need to buy any food for the family. I could use that money to get high. You're catching on now.

Cockeyed Junior

Cockeyed Junior came to my place with a tow truck.

"What's up, man? You're working as a tow truck driver now?"

"No, it's just transportation for today because I stole it."

I should have known it wasn't legit. "What are you trying to do?"

"I don't know."

"Remember that business center we saw in Virginia? Let's go hit some of those trucks."

We went out to Virginia and broke into a plumbing truck, stole all these tools out the back, put them in the truck, and we were ready to leave.

"Let's roll," I said as we got in and closed the doors.

Cockeyed Junior started the truck and then his eyes got big at something ahead of us. "You see that?"

I thought it was the police. "See what?"

"That race car. I have to get it."

"Man, we ain't got time for that! We got all this stolen stuff. We're going to get paid. Let's get out of here."

"No, man. I gotta get this car."

His mind was made up and he was driving, so I went along with him. "Come on, man. Let's hurry up and get it then."

We backed up the tow truck and lowered the tow to steal the car, and just when we were about to jump out, the police pulled up on us – a state trooper. He walked over to us, and we tried to keep our cool.

"May I have your manifest?" he asked.

Manifest? We didn't know what the heck he was talking about?

Cockeyed Junior said, "What do you want?"

"Your manifest – the papers authorizing you to get this car – your manifest."

Cockeyed Junior looked to me and whispered, "Man, we don't have no time. We have to run for it."

What? Run?! Before I knew what was going on, Cockeyed Junior shifted to *Drive* and floored it. The tow was dragging on the road and sparks were flying behind us. Right behind the sparks was the state trooper. We made it onto the highway and the truck started barking.

"What's that noise?!" I asked anxiously.

"We're out of gas! It was on *E* when I stole it."

"Why didn't you stop and get gas??" I asked with frustration.

"I didn't have any money."

"Why didn't you tell me so that I could put some gas in it?"

"I don't know."

We were so gung ho on stealing that we never went to get gas. I looked in the mirror and the trooper had backup with him.

Cockeyed Junior pulled off on the ramp and jumped out while the truck was still running! I wasn't as crazy as him, so I sat there waiting for the truck to stop so I could get out. When the truck finally stopped, I jumped out and ran in the direction Cockeyed Junior was heading. I climbed the fence, but when I got to the top the police grabbed me and pulled me back. Man, those cops pulled out their nightsticks and beat me like I was a black piñata. They fractured three of my ribs and gave me a concussion. They beat me so badly that I was glad to get locked up.

The first thing I did in jail was find the baddest dude in there and I started talking to him. The guy was really religious, so to disarm him, I started a prayer service in there. It worked like a charm! We were praising the Lord and having a good time.

The first time I went to court the police didn't show up. The second time, they didn't show up. They finally took me to a separate room and sat me down.

"We don't really want you. We want the guy driving the truck. What's his name?"

"Cockeyed Junior."

"What's his real name?"

"Cockeyed Junior."

They showed me a picture of him.

"Yeah, that's Cockeyed Junior."

"What's his real name?"

"I don't know. We call him Cockeyed Junior. See the picture... how one eye is looking one way and the other eye has something different on its mind? Cockeyed Junior."

I was happy to hear Cockeyed Junior got away.

On the third day, Kathy came to visit me in jail. This was the second time I was locked up.

"I ain't coming back to see you," she said.

I thought she was joking because she came to see me a lot the first time I got locked up, but she never came back. I told my father about her not coming to see me.

"I ain't coming back, either," my father said with a stern expression. "I told you, three strikes and you're out."

I knew he meant what he said. It was a lonely feeling in there for the next three months. Finally, the third court date approached and the police didn't show up.

"You're a lucky man," the defending attorney said to me and shook my hand.

"Why? What's going on?" I asked confused.

"You're free to go."

"Just like that?"

"Yes," she laughed. "Just like that."

"Thank you. How do I get home? I don't have any money."

"I have a card. You can catch the train home."

I took the card, caught the train, and ran all the way from that station to my apartment. I hit the intercom excited.

"Kathy! Kathy! Open the door! It's Russell!"

"How did you get out of jail?"

"They let me out, baby! I'm home!"

I was so happy to see her and the kids! I was back... and ready to get high.

CHAPTER EIGHTEEN

Bless The House

I had a friend named Berry I met in a crack house. He ended up staying with us for a while. He had a buddy named CJ that came over all the time. CJ was a metro bus driver. The first thing CJ would do when he came in was see if we had any food because he knew we didn't. He'd then take us to the store and buy us go groceries while Berry watched the kids. We'd come back to the house; he'd give me some money, and I'd go buy some crack for us. I was usually the one buying the crack because I knew the dealers. I'd go out there at 2 in the morning to score and the dealers would be waiting on me.

Anyway, you had to 'bless the house'--give us something--before you could smoke in our place. I told everybody from day one, "You have to bless the house first before you can bless the pipe," and every time afterwards, they did it automatically. And you couldn't give us just anything. Oh no, we didn't like those small blessings. We liked those Creflo

Dollar-sized blessings. I had to make sure I had enough for Kathy and me to smoke later.

When I returned with the crack, CJ always wanted the first hit, because he knew like all crackheads do that the first hit of a rock is the killer. He'd give me $50 for a rock, but they were slightly bigger than usual because I had the 'pancake rock' hookup from the Jamaicans. We called the big $50 rocks "workers." I was 'the taxer.' I'd cut that baby down to the size of a regular 50 and slide it in my pocket. And since it was so big, no one would miss anything.

I'd cut, CJ would get the first hit. He'd get up, walk around, then leave the room and go into the living room and plunk down on the couch. As soon as his butt hit that couch, Kathy and I grabbed that pipe and smoked the hell out of that rock. Then he'd come back into the room.

"Psst. Russell, the police is outside."

I'd go to the window and look down into the parking lot. "Man, ain't nobody outside."

He'd go back into the living room and sit on the couch. He'd return a few minutes later.

"That was a good hit," he said. "Anymore left?"

"Nah, it's all gone."

Puff, Puff, Run!

Jason, our selling-weed-out-of-a-mobile-home-neighbor, had two apartments on the main floor of the building. One day, I was on a snooping mission near the one he used to store his weed. I saw a big bowl in the kitchen overflowing with weed. I tried to open that damn window, but it was locked.

I have to get my hands on some of that weed!, I said to myself.

Since I couldn't sneak in through the window, I walked into the building and knocked on the door. Ms. Carlita opened it.

I put on my angel face. "Hey, Ms. Carlita. May I use your phone?"

"Come on in. You can use the phone. It's right in the kitchen."

I grabbed the phone and acted like I was talking. "Hey baby, do you know where I placed my keys? I can't find them anywhere," I said as I was shoving weed in my pocket. Jason wouldn't miss it because he had pounds of it. I hit the block and sold that weed in a few minutes.

When you got a good thing, you keep going back. I kept going back. Every few days, I'd go down there to use the phone. Then she changed up on me.

"Hey, Ms. Carlita, may I use your phone?"

"No, you can't use my phone no more."

"Huh?" I said confused. "What happened?"

"You just can't use the phone anymore."

Jason realized everything was coming up short, and he knew Ms. Carlita wasn't stealing. He asked her who'd been in there, and she told him I came in there a couple of time to use the phone. Sayonara, Ms. Carlita, it was fun while it lasted.

Hook Me Up Chuck

A dealer named Chuck sent somebody to get me as I was actually on my way down to Anacostia to buy some crack. I had $50. I went with Chuck's henchman to a vacant house that Chuck was selling out of. There were candles everywhere.

"Hey, man," I said to the Chuck. "What's up? I need a 50."

He gave me a working 50. "I need you to hook the electricity up in here so I can have some lights."

I said, "I can take care of that if you give me something worthwhile."

"I'll give you some after you cut them on."

That's all I needed to hear. I went and got two nails, put them in the meter, and got the lights back on. I went back inside.

"Thanks, Russ. You're the man."

"You're welcome."

He handed me some bags. "Look, from now on, whatever you got, you come down here and I'll take care of you."

"Thanks, man." I stepped out the door and began walking home. I looked down and counted the rocks and it turns out he gave me $100 worth of crack. *And the winner is*! I didn't expect that much. I wasn't walking no more – I sprinted home like 'The Flash' to Kathy.

"Baby, I hit the jackpot!" I said as I showed her the crack.

She jumped in my arms like we just won the mega-millions lottery. We got high all night!

The next day, Chuck sent somebody to come get me again.

"Russ, I need some guns."

"I'll see what I can do," I said as the wheels in my head began turning.

"Whatever you get, I'll buy them on the spot."

I immediately tracked down two of my cousins and told them we were going to break into a pawnshop and steal some guns. We rode down Bladensburg Road to the pawnshop and tried to break in the back door. It wouldn't budge. Just as we were giving up, Hawaii five-oh came outta nowhere.

"What are you all doing out here?" they asked.

"We just came here to use the bathroom; we'd been drinking."

The officer eyed each of us suspiciously. "Get out of here."

We left… sans guns.

Pook, a stone-cold dealer, and his boys came to our house with a proposition.

"Russ, I need to house some stuff at your crib for a bit." This was a rough dude that was always packing heat. I didn't want no parts of it.

"I'm sorry, you can't come in here with guns. We got kids."

"I don't have any guns. I just want to keep some product here. Cool?"

It was going to cost him. "As long as you bless the house."

"Of course, we can do that."

They blessed us with a nice amount of crack. Kathy and I had a good time smoking it all up, and we didn't have to spend any money or go out and hustle to get it.

They were checking in every other day, but suddenly, they left and didn't come back for weeks. We started cleaning up the apartment, and I began snooping to find out where they hid their stuff. I know they left something behind, but I couldn't find out where. Any dealer that uses a person's house always has something they're going to stash for later.

I kept searching, and finally, there it was – a gun in the closet hidden way in the back on a shelf. I instantly thought about Chuck. I took the gun to him and he gave me a big ol' rock. Kathy and I hit the jackpot again! And those dudes never knew what hit 'em.

Minimum Crack Wage

When you're on drugs, people will work you for crackhead wages. What's the crackhead wage? Twenty funky dollars. Yes, $20. You'd work hours upon hours doing some of the roughest task known to mankind. At the end of the day, you were given $20. And crack has such a hold on an addict; they'll do anything to get that $20. I was fortunate to be a professional electrician, but I wasn't getting paid like it. I was earning crackhead wages like every other crackhead. My uncle Norman would come pick me up to do electrical work, and he'd work me all day for $20. He'd take me to somebody's house. I'd put lights up, fix appliances, run wiring throughout the house, and whatever else he needed me to do. At the end of the day he'd take me back home and give me $20. I was happy because I had something to bring to Kathy.

There was another guy named Lynn that owned a liquor store. And Lynn was another $20 man. I used to do electrical work at his store for hours at a time and he'd pay me $20.

But that all changed when I saw him take the daily money from the register and put it in the bag under the register in the back of the store. Often, I'd be left unattended because Lynn had vouched for me with his employees. They trusted me. So, I would do a little work, sneak around back, put a little money in my pocket, then get back to work. At the end of the night, Lynn would pick me up and take me home. He'd give me $20 and I'd add that to all the money I took that day. He never suspected a thing.

But crack addiction is a monster. You'll do anything to get the money to chase those rocks – even bite the hand that feeds you. One time, Lynn had just put all the money he made that day in his car. On his way to drop me back home, we stopped at a laundromat and he started talking to this girl inside. Knowing he'd be distracted for a good minute, I went back to the parking lot and tried to break into his car to get that bag of money. Just as I found the lock's sweet spot, he caught me.

"What are you doing, Russell?"

I was caught red-handed and knew there was no way to bullshit my way out of this one. I may have been a crackhead, but I was an honest one. I had to come clean because he trusted me. ""I was trying to break in and get the money."

He could've killed me right then and there because he had a gun on him, but he knew I was a victim of the rock. Saddened and disappointed, he shook his head and never took me back to his store again.

Three-Way Calling

Crackheads don't pay bills. And with all my money going to cop drugs, it's no wonder my phone got disconnected. But handy crackheads like myself are also super resourceful. And I had a bright idea to get our phone cut back on. I was going to connect my line to our neighbor Jason's apartment – even though he lived on an entirely different floor! I ran my phone line along the outside of the building from upstairs all the way downstairs to his. And bam!, three-way calling crackhead style! Can you hear me now?

I told people, "Look, if you have to make a phone call and you hear somebody pickup – hang up quick. If there's a dial tone, go on and make a call." Well, one day, this dude I didn't really know was talking on the phone and when Jason got on the phone, this fool kept talking!

"Hello?" Jason asked.

"Hello?"

"Who is this?"

"This Mike."

Jason was pissed! "Mike, what the hell are you doing on my phone? How did you get on here?"

People kept calling us on that line and it would drive Jason crazy because he didn't know what was going on. He'd pick up the phone and hear people already in mid-conversation. He thought a party line was interfering with his line. Confused and frustrated, he called the phone company and cursed them out. I know how it went down because I was listening to their conversation!

The phone company came out.

"Well, we found the problem."

"Y'all messed up! That's the problem!" Jason said indignantly.

"It wasn't us. You have a neighbor upstairs that tapped into your line so that you two shared the same line. Here it is." He showed Jason the wire I ran down the wall and traced the line right to my apartment.

Jason looked at me. "You know something about this?"

"What is that?" I asked playing stupid.

"It's a phone line," he said and threw it at me.

I caught it and looked at it. "I don't know what this is," and threw it back at him.

"You ain't know nothing about this?"

"No, I ain't know nothing about this."

Crackhead rule #2,144 – Deny, Deny, Deny! I marched into my apartment and slammed the door.

Kathy's father stopped by one day and Jason made sure to let him know what I'd done, "If I didn't know that was your daughter, I would've killed her boyfriend." I'm sure Kathy's father wanted to tell Jason, "Please, don't let knowing me stop you."

CHAPTER NINETEEN

Ma, Loan Me Some Money

Kathy used to walk a couple miles to her parents' house to get money from her mother. Her mother was looking out for her before her father even knew she was on drugs. She worked at Drug Fair, which was a drug store like CVS. Kathy would go there when she knew she was working.

"Mama, the kids need pampers."

"If the kids need pampers, then go on back there and get what you need."

Kathy would get the pampers and her mother would pay for them.

Many times, her mother brought money and food to our apartment. She was always sweet, but even the sweetest woman has her limits. Kathy went over to her parents' house one evening.

"Mama, I need a couple of dollars. Can you loan me—"

"I ain't loaning y'all no more money! And let me tell you something – y'all got the pissiest kids I've ever seen!"

"But, Mama—"

"Mama my ass! I ain't giving y'all no more of my damn money!"

Kathy's mom didn't want to be an enabler, but she felt sorry for her daughter. She still ended up sliding Kathy a few dollars. And it was like that from that day on – she'd tell Kathy she wasn't giving her any money, then give her $10 or $20. What's crazy is that Kathy used to be the one doing all the loaning. She was the one who always loaned her sister and her mother money, but now all she did was borrow money from them and never paid them back. That's when Kathy knew she was doing badly. That's when she knew crack had gotten the best of her.

Public Assistance

Kathy resigned from her job after our son was born. She told them she had to take care of our kids, but she really did it to get herself together. Our home had become a crackhouse – all manner of strangers traipsing through at all hours of the day, the fridge and cabinets were almost always barren and the bills piled up like Mt. Everest. Who had she become? And how was she going to straighten out this mess that had become her life? Earnest's sister had an idea.

"You should get on Public Assistance."

"Oh no," Kathy said and shook her head.

"I'm serious. They'll give you money for rent, give you food, and you don't have to pay them back."

Kathy secretly looked down on those welfare women. She may have been a crackhead, but at least she wasn't on food stamps. But having no other choice, she reluctantly went down there, only to be turned away. She told Earnest's sister what happened.

"Did you go down there?"

"Yeah, but they said I didn't qualify."

"What? You need to go back down there and tell them nobody's helping you and you ain't got nothing. Go back down there."

Kathy visited the welfare office again and pleaded her case. This time, the people wanted to know who the father of her children was. But Kathy was gangster with it. She wouldn't tell them a damn thing, so they put her through the wringer. Next, they wanted a copy of her bank account and her W-2. Man, those employees acted as if it was their money they were giving to her.

Eventually, they gave her food stamps and helped with our rent. The rent help was the worst for her because Kathy was still prideful. She hated having to wait every month for that little check to come in the mail. The rent wasn't but $300! And she loathed being on food stamps. She'd go and get the food, but she always saved some food stamps to sell. You'd only get half the amount of the money when you sold them. If you found somebody that would pay you more, you'd *always* go to that person first. Sometimes, she'd get drug dealers to take food stamps. I don't know how she did it, but she did. That was rough for her, but she continued to battle to get clean and to stay clean.

The Prodigal Daughter

Kathy:

When my daughter was around 2-years old, she began running her mouth in ways I didn't foresee. It happened when one of our friends came over and picked up my homemade pipe off the coffee table.

My daughter said, "That's my mommy's binky." How in the hell did she know what that was!

That was my breaking point. When I heard that, I said, *Kathy, it's time to stop smoking and get yourself together.* Whether Russell was going to get himself together or not, I was going to get clean for my kids' sake. I wasn't brought up like that, so I knew better. And no one in my family was on drugs, which meant I was the drug addict of the family. On top of that, the rent wasn't paid, and I knew we couldn't get put out on the street. So, I did the thing I hated doing most, I called my parents.

"Mama, can I move back home?" I knew she was going to say yes.

My mother said, "Let me ask your father."

She was trying to scare me. Then my father got on the phone.

"Let me think about it."

Calmly and in the sweetest voice I could muster, I said, "Okay, Daddy," but inside I was going off! *What?! You have to think about it? I ain't going to have anywhere to stay! Had I fallen so far that my own parents won't take me back?*

My mind was racing. I was about to lose it when my father said, "You can come back, but don't bring anything back with you. Just you, your kids, and your clothes."

I packed a dresser full of the kids' clothes and my clothes. Then I went to say bye to Russell.

"Bye, Russell."

"See ya," he said as if I was going to work.

And just like that, I moved out.

It was nice when I got home. I loved the break away from all the craziness. Everything was quiet and there weren't lots of people coming to the house all day. The first night I went to bed, I got on my knees and asked God to take the taste of crack away from me. I prayed for Him to take the drugs away from me and deliver me. I guess He heard me because suddenly, I became laser-focused. I'd think about crack every now and then, but I knew I was on the road to sobriety. It was really what I wanted to do. I was able to gradually pull my life back together. I kept myself busy, and my kids kept me busy. I fed them breakfast, cleaned them, took them out, washed up after them, got them ready for school, cooked them lunch, and made them dinner. I had a lot of making up to do and tending to them kept me busy. Thank God.

The two main goals of getting myself back together were going to church and rebuilding my credit. I didn't have a car or a license. I was still getting food stamps and public assistance. That was a blessing to my parents because I paid the rent and bought food for the house.

I started being around my family and friends more often. Some of them smoked weed, but I wasn't into that anyway, so I didn't care. I just had a good time eating and having a little drink from time to time. I used to visit my neighbor and that helped a lot too because my kids could run around and play. I needed to disassociate myself from all the people I got high with – including Russell.

Last Man Standing

Kathy decided she wanted to leave out the clear blue. After all those years, she decided she had enough, and I didn't see it coming. There I was all by myself. The only bright side was I didn't have to share my crack with her, but I missed her. I was all alone. But that didn't last long. Remember the neighbors that moved in with their kids and then moved out when the lights got cut off? Well, they were walking by at night and saw that my lights were on, which meant I had *electricity*. They came upstairs to see me and never left.

I stayed in the apartment because I didn't have anywhere to go. I didn't pay the rent, but I was going to stay there until they put me out. Until then, I was going to keep hustling, keep getting high, and enjoying myself.

I was in the back room getting high with Charley, a childhood friend, when I heard the door open.

"Who's there?" Charley asked me.

"I think they're here to evict me."

That crack had both of us paranoid. I stepped out the room and saw Kathy. She was looking good, too. She kind of took me back to when we met.

"Hey, Kathy," I said while trying to act like I wasn't getting high. "What are you doing here? You moving back?"

"No. My mother drove me here so I could get my mail."

"It's in the kitchen in the drawer by the refrigerator."

"Thank you. Just keep doing what y'all are doing back there."

She was inferring that we were getting high. She could see it on my face and smell it in the air. She grabbed her mail and walked right out before I could really talk to her. It had been a month since I saw her, and she probably saw the old lifestyle she used to live and wanted no part of it.

I didn't see Kathy for another few weeks, but I kept it moving. My hustles suffered a drought so all I could do was sell stuff. I already sold the vacuum cleaner and the dining room set. I looked around the apartment for something to sell. When I found something, I hit the block.

"Hey, you want to buy this?" I asked the first person I walked by. He said "Hell no." I walked to a group of people. "Y'all want to buy this?" They looked at me like I was on crack… and I wasn't even high yet! None of them wanted it. I kept it moving. Suddenly, I spotted Kathy's sister Renee.

"Hey, don't you need one of these?" I asked her.

"Russell, you're out here trying to sell a kitchen counter?"

"This thing is nice," I told her as I struggled to set it down. Before I could begin to give her my infomercial sales pitch, she barked, "I don't want it." So I kept asking around. Thirty minutes later, there was Kathy, shaking her head in pity and disgust.

"Russell! That's the apartment's counter. You can't sell that. If you do, they're going to hold me responsible and you'll mess up my credit…again!"

I didn't want to hurt her any more than I already had. Despite how much I needed my next high, I cared for Kathy more, so I put it back.

Dealing With Daddy

Kathy:

My father watched me. He wouldn't say much, but he watched me like a hawk to see if I was clean. He didn't want me hanging out and he wouldn't allow me to have any company over. I cooked dinner every night and started getting on a totally new program. I'd take the kids for walks and nice things like that. My father would say, "If you aren't strong enough, it will make you go back out there and smoke that stuff." My father was a jokester. One time, I came into the kitchen and there were these little white specks all over the floor. They looked like crack rocks. I looked closer and realized they were small pieces of bread. Just then, my dad walked in with a sly smile on his face. "Funny, Dad. Real funny." I knew he was proud of me and my sisters. He called us his "blessings."

My blessing was I didn't have to go to rehab. My blessing was I came to their house and got myself together. Maybe their house was my rehab and my blessing. I don't know. But it wasn't easy. My father treated me like a rehab patient in the beginning. One time, he really hurt my feelings as I walked by he and his friends.

"Hey, Daddy," I greeted him.

"Hey, baby," he said and then looked to his friends. "That's my rehab patient."

I couldn't believe he said that. I was so hurt and humiliated. I couldn't get over it because he would say it a lot when people came over. It was hard enough without having to be constantly reminded of my struggle. It wasn't helping and I'd had enough. I found my mother in the house.

"Mommy, you have to talk to Daddy."

"Why? What's going on?"

"He tells his friends that I'm his rehab patient. I'm not his rehab patient. I'm his daughter."

"He knows you're his daughter."

"He doesn't act like it. What he needs to realize is I'm doing this because I want to do it, not because he wants me to do it. Tell him I'd appreciate it if he stopped saying that."

She must have talked to him because he stopped saying it. If I weren't strong at this point, I could've got down on myself and went back out there and started smoking crack again. But by the grace of God, I was delivered from it. I'm not going to lie; the thought of smoking crack always came to my mind. Sometimes it came in a dream. Other times, I'd smell it. That's the addiction.

I drank sometimes a little bit every blue moon. My father had liquor in the house, but I never touched it. I always waited until my mother came home and had a drink with her, but I never drank when they weren't around. My father would say he was leaving, then he'd leave and come back ten minutes later, go in the basement, and check to see if I was still doing drugs. He never found anything because I never did anything. He definitely saw the change in me. I knew he was proud, but he just never said it.

No Russell Allowed

Kathy:

My father absolutely hated Russell, so once I moved back, to his house, he didn't want to see Russell and he certainly couldn't come over.

I'd say, "Daddy, can Russell—"

Before his name even left my lips, he'd cut me off.

"No. I don't want Russell around here."

It made me feel bad because I wanted Russell to at least see his kids. We threw a birthday party at my parents' house for our son. Russell came over to celebrate. But as soon as my father looked out the window and saw Russell, he bolted out of there with the quickness.

"You have to go!"

"Go where?" Russell asked.

"It doesn't matter as long as it's off my property."

Russell was hurt, and I felt bad for him. I walked him out of the yard. When we got there, Russell turned around.

"I can't believe he won't let me stay at my own child's birthday party."

"I know how you feel, and I feel bad that you can't stay, but this is his house."

"I know it's his house, but why's he so worried about me when he's got the biggest crook in the backyard?"

"Who? David?"

"No, you!"

I laughed so hard, they could hear me in the backyard.

"No, baby, I'm just kidding. I'm not talking about you being a crook. I'm talking about your sister's boyfriend and his friend." Russell's smile had faded to seriousness. He might still be on that rock, but Russell also knew about everything going down in the streets. I made sure to keep a closer eye on my sister's company from then on.

I don't know if it was because of me and the kids, his ingrained upbringing or him wanting to try and get straight on his own, but eventually, Russell started going back to church. Still, it was too little, too late. No matter what he did bad or good, my father still didn't want him around.

CHAPTER TWENTY

Eviction Day

I heard them put eviction papers on the door. And when I saw them, I knew the party was officially over. I had a good run in that apartment, but it was time to move on. I called my sister, Linda, and she came right over. She was a blessing, though she probably felt obligated to help me because I took her and her baby in long before I was totally cracked out. But still, she really helped me out.

"Russell, you can stay with me."

"Thank the Lord."

"Just bring a little bit of your stuff," she said.

That was easy because all I had was a little bit of stuff. Most of my clothes were dirty, so I put my underwear, t-shirts, and a pair of pants in a little bag and walked out the door with her. When I moved out, there were guys still in my back room getting high, but I just closed the apartment door and left them there. I wanted to get high with them, but I had to move on.

When they came the next day to evict me, I was gone. They really couldn't evict anything because there was nothing inside to evict except the guys I left there getting high. When Kathy left, I basically sold everything I could carry for crack.

The first day at Linda's place, she said, "Russell you can stay here, but don't do drugs in my house, blah, blah, blah." I smiled and nodded pretending to listen. She cooked me and her son dinner; we talked, and had a good time. I followed the rules and didn't get high in her house that night... but it was only because I didn't have any money.

Soon, I met a pastor and his wife and I gave them my sister's number to get in touch with me if they ever needed any work done. They knew I was on drugs because I was straight up with them, but they called me and hired me to do electrical work. They would come and get me all the time, I'd work for them, and they'd drop me off at the end of the day. On one occasion, they said, "We're going to take you downstairs and pray for you." They continued on, "We're going to preach to you, pray for you, and we're going to give you the Holy Ghost." Give me? Now, that didn't sound right. I remember the preacher always said the Holy Ghost is something you get – nobody can just give it to you. But I went along with the program. They were down there praying and screaming over me. I didn't really care because all I wanted to do was get paid, go home, and get some crack, so whatever it took for me to be taken home was fine with me.

When I got some money, the first thing I did was get high in my sister's house. It turns out that the girl downstairs from her sold drugs. Merry Crackmas to me! I knew she was selling by the type of people that were stopping by. Druggies know druggies and we always know when something is going on. We can sniff it out like crack-hounds. If someone was selling crack or doing it, oh, you best believe I'd know it soon.

She was like a gay tomboy and really nice, but I knew something was going on in there. I just had to get myself in the door. Once I got myself in, I used to get high all the time. She'd let me smoke on credit, and I always paid her. I'd say, "Let me get a 20 or a 50," then I'd go back upstairs and get high. When I was getting high, I had to look out of the blinds for my sister because she used to come home every day at the same time. I could see her car coming down the street. Whenever I saw it, I'd start cleaning up and try to act like I wasn't high.

She'd say, "What are you doing?"

"Nothing. Just cleaning up."

One time, my sister had a party, and Kathy came. I wasn't high that night because I had to put up a front like I was getting myself together. But Kathy could see right through me.

"Russell, you're high."

"No, I'm not," I lied.

"Yes, you are."

"How do you know that?"

"I can tell by how you talk."

"I ain't getting high. You know my tooth is still missing from that fight I got into. That's why I sound funny."

"That's not it. I can tell by how you talk because your voice is slurred."

"I ain't getting high."

"Yes, you are. I'm going to tell Linda."

And Kathy sure did snitch on me.

"I think your brother is still getting high."

"He is?"

"Yes, I can hear it in his voice"

Linda immediately came to my room accusing me, "Are you still getting high?"

I denied it, but she didn't believe me because of what Kathy told her. I can't believe Kathy told on me. Ain't that something?

With Relatives Like Me, You Don't Need Enemies

Before long, stuff at my sister's house began coming up missing: rings, money, and even her car. I stole her car every night when she went to sleep. She'd leave the keys in the kitchen and I'd take them. I'd go buy crack and come back home. I'd go to my mother or my uncles and tell them I needed a few dollars, and they'd usually give me some. But I think I went to my uncle's house one too many times. He got tired of me borrowing money *he knew* I wasn't going to pay back.

"Unc," I said as he answered the door.

"What's up?"

"I need some money, man. I have to pay these drug guys! They said if I don't pay them they're going to kill me."

He looked me square in my eyes and said, "Been nice knowing you. *You* told them *you'd* pay them, so *you* pay them. But you won't be paying them with my money." And he slammed the door in my face.

It was tough love, but I respected him for that. After that, he would always come and get me to do electrical work. If he was going to give me money, I'd have to earn it. And thank goodness my trade always got me some money.

Geekin'

My sister Linda's boyfriend, Contee, was a DC cop. Whenever he came over to chill, she'd always ask him to talk to me in hopes that maybe he could talk me off the rock.

"You need to talk to my brother," she said. "He's in there going crazy."

He came in my room. I was butt naked.

"He's alright," he told my sister. "He's just geekin'."

He came back to my room and stood at the door. I tried to act like I didn't see him.

"Hey, Russell, put on some drawers, man. And hurry up."

I put some drawers on, and then he sat down.

"You're hurting your sister, man. You need to get yourself together."

"I know, man. I know."

"She deserves respect. All she wants to do is help you, and you keep messing up."

"I know, man. You're right." I acted remorseful, but inside I was saying, *I wish he would hurry up and get out of here. He's blowing my high.*

The High Hero

Kathy brought the kids over one Sunday, but I was exhausted from being up all night getting high. My 2-year-old son, Rakeem, was playing on the balcony and dropped his toy through the bars three-stories down. He then squeezed through the bars to get it and got stuck. Kathy was so skinny and frail, she couldn't pick him up.

"Go wake up your daddy!" she told our daughter as she ran downstairs to catch our son.

My daughter barged into my room screaming, "Daddy! Daddy, get up!"

I wouldn't budge.

"Daddy! Daddy!" she kept screaming.

Finally I got up and went with her. That's when I saw my son hanging onto the balcony by his little hand and foot. I ran to the balcony and pulled him over the rail. Kathy was petrified. I was, too. I almost lost my son forever. That shook me up so bad, I called the elder at the church to come pray for us. He prayed for me, my wife, son, and daughter. You'd think that was enough to scare me straight and make me stop getting high, but it wasn't.

Time's Up

After that scare, I began doing right. I got a job and I wasn't smoking as much as I used to. I was doing a lot better. But I slipped and ended up taking my sister's ring. She always set her ring on the dresser, and I always walked by it looking at it. Eventually, I took the ring and sold it for $100 to the dealer downstairs and I also took some money she had saved up for her son. My sister was fed up. She went downstairs and knocked on the tomboy drug dealer's door.

"Yes?" the dealer said.

"You know what? I don't know you, but I'd really appreciate it if you stopped selling my brother drugs."

"I don't sell drugs," she told my sister.

"Stop selling my brother drugs."

"Who is your brother?"

"Russell."

That was the beginning of the end. That dealer never let me inside nor sold me any more crack.

When I came home that day, my bag was by the door. What's up with the bag? Wait, it was my bag. I knocked on the door. Linda opened it.

"Yes."

"Why is my bag out here?"

"I'm done. You have to go."

"I don't have anywhere to go."

"Yes, you do. You can live with Sharon."

Oh, Lord! Sharon was one of our sisters, the meanest one of all, and she didn't play. I'd rather go back to prison than stay with Sharon. *Dang it, Russ, you messed up a good thing.*

CHAPTER TWENTY-ONE

Get It Together, Russell

Getting kicked out of Linda's place and sent to Sharon's was the best thing that ever happened to me. Sharon had two daughters, so I slept in the living room. What was funny was when I went to church all the time when I was younger, Sharon wouldn't go, but I kept trying to get her to go. Now, when I moved in with her, she was going to church all the time and I wasn't going at all. However, I thank God I grew up in the church because it made me stayed prayed up. I prayed every night, even in my darkest hour, and that connection to the Lord made it easy to get back into church.

I knew it was time to give up crack. My family suggested I go to rehab, but my father was against it. He would always say, "Rehab ain't get you on drugs, and rehab ain't getting you off drugs."

On the first day I stayed with Sharon, she went to work and the kids went to school. There I was, all alone in her house desperately trying to ignore every urge I had to steal because if Sharon kicked me out, I knew was a goner. She was my last hope. I dropped to my knees and prayed with the fervor of Reverend Ike.

"Lord, if you take this addiction from me, I will do right. Please, take this addiction from me. I come to you baring my heart and my soul. Everything I have belongs to you. Only you have the power to take this addiction from me. I will not give any more power to the devil…"

I don't know how long I prayed, but when I got up, I was delivered. One thing for sure is when you make up your mind and you believe in your heart that you're changing, the devil cannot stop you. I didn't even have a taste for drugs anymore – the burden was taken away.

I got a job over an hour away in Gaithersburg, and I didn't have a car, but I was so dedicated and determined that I couldn't be stopped from getting there. I had to get up early in the morning and babysit for my sister, Fuzzy, until 4am, then I would catch the train when the first train left the terminal all the way downtown. From there, I transferred to Gaithersburg, which was the last stop on the line. Then I had to catch a train from there to the job site. Getting to work was a job unto itself, and I took that trek every morning before the sun rose for two months.

While on a job site I came across a wallet. I picked it up and there was $200 inside. That's when the old familiar voice crept up on me.

"Russell?"

"I know what you're going to say, and the answer is no," I rebuked.

"Don't fight the feeling, Russell. This free money is a sign for you to go get high. You can get high tonight. Just put the money in your pocket."

I ignored it – I didn't want drugs anymore. I looked past the money and credit cards, and got the name of the person it belonged to: Chad Stephenson, a young, white guy that operated heavy equipment. I went to the guy.

"Here's your wallet."

He didn't even know he had lost it. He felt his back pockets and then took the wallet. "Where did you find it?"

"Over there by the door. You don't have to worry, all your money is there."

He looked at it and counted it. When I was leaving to go catch the train at the end of the day, he came over to me.

"Where do you live?" he asked.

"I have to catch the train to New Carrollton."

"I go past that way every day. If you want, you can ride with me every day to work and I'll drop you off after work."

That opportunity happened because I did right and I knew it was God rewarding me. And He didn't stop there.

I met another guy on the job named Phil, a painter/drywaller. We were eating lunch and he told me he lived in Largo. I told him I lived in Suitland, Maryland. He said, "I have a car that I can give you if you pay the mechanic that fixed it."

"For real?"

"Yeah, pay him and it's yours for free. I'll take you down there if you want me to."

True to his word, I paid the mechanic $600. Blessing #2.

And guess what? Just like my Dad, I kept my car extra clean. One day, the owner of the business, named Melvin, walked right up to me.

"You keep a nice-looking car."

"You want me to clean yours?"

"Would you?"

I cleaned the owner's car and he gave me $100. He loved his "new" car.

"From now on, you're my detail man," he said as he smiled at it. Blessing #3.

Whenever work slacked up, I'd give Melvin's car a special wash and wax. When work dried up and they laid us off, he'd take me and a couple of guys to his house and we'd cut the grass, trim the hedges, and help out however and wherever we could. No matter what happened, God provided.

I found a job closer to home, so I was leaving Melvin's job site. Melvin said, "Russell, if you ever need work, you can always come back here."

The next thing I knew, I had a truck, a cell phone to go with my new job, side jobs, and my sobriety. God was making things happen in my life – all I had to do was ask.

A New Beginning

Kathy and I had been working on our relationship, and finally it was returning to the healthy relationship we had before crack invaded our lives. We rented a small two-bedroom house that divided a fork in the road. We called it our 'Little House On The Prairie.' If someone got drunk and didn't turn left or right, they'd end up tearing our whole house down. It was so small that my daughter and son, who were in their early years of elementary school, had to room together. It was no big deal to me because I grew up sleeping with my brother in our living room, but apparently it was too close for comfort for those two. One night I heard screaming. I ran in to find my son walking around with his eyes closed and my daughter crying.

"What's going on in here?"

My son said, "I don't know. I was eating pizza and she began screaming."

My daughter yelled, "That not pizza, that's my foot!"

I shook my son, and his eyes opened. "Are you awake?"

"Where am I?"

"You're in the hallway, boy!"

"We weren't just eating pizza?"

"Nobody was eating pizza unless you were having a pepperoni and foot pizza! Now apologize to your sister."

We laughed it off and I put them back to bed. I told Kathy about our son's shenanigans and she just laughed.

The next morning, Kathy and I were on our way to the babysitter's house to pick up the kids.

"What kind of car do you want?" I asked her.

"Something like that little blue Toyota right there," she said as she pointed to a car parked outside the babysitter's house.

I went inside and said, "Who owns that little blue Toyota out there?"

"I do," a woman said that was picking up her kids.

"I'll buy it from you right now."

"You know what?" she smiled. "I'm actually leaving town and have been trying to sell it."

"For real?"

"Yeah."

That's all I needed to hear. "Let's go look at it." It looked fine and I bought it on the spot. Then I looked at Kathy. "You wanted that car. Well, it's yours now." And I didn't have to steal it!

We took it home, and now we had *two cars* and a truck when a few months back, we had nothing. Soon I bought another truck. Then my older son's mother was having problems with him and sent him to live with me. I had my entire family together for the first time in forever. Life got so good that everything I touched turned to gold. I knew as long as I kept my word, God would keep His. God's favor was on us.

To Love, Honor, and Respect

From the time I got on my knees and got back into the church, my entire paradigm shifted in a major way. I wasn't ripping and running anymore. I was drug-free and I was more in love with Kathy than ever before. I thought about all that we went through, all the good times and a lot of the bad times. I vowed we would never go any lower than where we were ever again. All we could do was go up. And it was time to take things to the next level.

So I gave Kathy an ultimatum. "Kathy, either we're going to get married or you're going to have to leave and let me find someone else because I don't want to be living in sin no more. I'm trying to do the right thing."

Kathy hesitated.

"Are you scared of getting married?"

"No," she said. "I'm scared of marrying you."

"What?"

"Russell, do you know how much you put me through? You can be downright crazy sometimes."

I smiled. She was totally right. But I reassured her, "All that stuff is so far in the past that there's no need in worrying about it. I'm a changed man and I love you."

We decided to get married. I began talking about how we could plan our wedding and who could do this and that for us at the church. Kathy stopped me.

"You know what, Russell? I don't need them to do anything. Let's just get married when we get the license."

Whatever my queen says, that's what we were going to do. We went to church and got counseling, and I told them the sooner we could get married, the better. After we completed counseling, they gave us a wedding date f*or that Wednesday!*

We called all of our family and friends and said the same thing, "Russell and I are getting married. It's going to be two days from now on Wednesday night at the church at 7:00pm." If you can make it...great. If not, we understood.

It was all a whirlwind, but we'd been together for 10 years. What did we need a big wedding for? We didn't have a bunch of money, but we had God, love, and a relationship being built on a new crack-free foundation and that was all we needed.

Kathy's father refused to come to the wedding. He fought it for those two days. When Wednesday night came, instead of coming into the church, he kept driving around the church with her mother – just circling the block over and over again.

"I don't know if I can do this," he kept telling Kathy's mother. "I don't want to give her away to him."

Her mother said, "Stop riding around this block and park so we can go in this church!"

I didn't know what was going on, but I knew her father still didn't like me. I told Kathy, "If your father isn't here in 10 more minutes, we're going to get married without him."

Kathy walked over to her cousin. "Nayboo, if Daddy doesn't hurry up, I'm going to need you to walk me down the aisle."

But just as he'd agreed, her father came bursting in with a scowl on his face. He wasn't happy at all. Not. At. All.

We're Movin' On Up

The program Kathy was in asked her where she wanted to work. She said HUD. She got a position there as an intern with a small stipend that correlated with the amount of hours she worked. They eventually offered her an entry-level job, so she took it to get her foot in the door.

We were doing really well. We both were settled, had jobs, and were making money. We put off buying a house, but God works in mysterious ways. We were at church, and the owner of our rental called us into the lobby and told us we had to move. We really didn't mind moving, but it was the middle of the school year and we didn't want the kids to have to change schools.

Someone I met sent me to a realtor that needed work done on a house. It was strange when I got there because I kept saying, *This house looks familiar. It reminds me of my grandmother's house.* Come to find out, it was my grandmother's house! We used to go down there every Sunday when I was a kid for Sunday dinner. What threw me off was that it now had a toilet *in* the house and heat. It didn't when my grandmother had it. They fixed it up so much that it was hard to tell. I told the lady it was my grandmother's house, then told her my wife and I had to move.

"How soon?" she asked.

"Real soon."

"I'll get right on it. In the meantime, I have another house I need you to do some work on in Oxon Hill."

I went up there and looked at the house. It was beautiful, but it was under contract. It had six bedrooms; it was in a nice neighborhood, and the school was right up the street. I did some work in there for her and she called me a week later.

"Mr. Thornton, the deal fell through on the house. I remember you said you like it. Would you be interested in buying it?"

"Yeah!"

"How much do you qualify for?"

I wasted no time jumping on that opportunity. I took my wife to look at it, and it was so much bigger than the two-bedroom house we were in. Now my daughter could have her own room and didn't have to worry about being mistaken for a slice of pepperoni pizza.

I got saved and cleaned my life up, and Lynn, the guy that owned the liquor store whose car I tried to break into, came to our housewarming. He was so proud of me. He bought us lots of wine. Not only did we become friends again, but he hired me to do work for him again. God is a miracle worker!

After 15 years of being there, we bought and moved into the house my uncle sold us – the uncle that made me turn myself in decades earlier. My sister Linda co-signed for the house and eventually moved in with us for a while.

I started going to church all the time and I prayed for Kathy's father all the time. I prayed that he would see the bigger picture and one day forgive me. He gave up on me years ago, but I wasn't going to give up on him.

Kathy's mother died, and her father got sick. I went to the hospital every day to pray for him. Before he died, he realized I was the man for his daughter. We were in the presence of lots of their family members and he placed his hand on my shoulder.

"This is my best son-in-law," he said.

That really warmed my heart. I finally had his respect.

Standing Strong

If you would've told me back then that Kathy and I would be where we are today, I would've thought you were on crack! But we're standing stronger than we ever imagined. I still work as an electrician, but now I <u>own</u> the business. Tolson Electric has been thriving for over 20 years and I truly love what I do.

As for Kathy, she still currently works in Human Resources, but she's too has her own passion and has launched her own a line of purses called 'KHARISMA.' They have style and grace just like the name… and her.

I could've been a success much sooner if I hadn't gone through the many ups and downs of addiction and could've saved myself and my family from so much heartache, embarrassment, and pain if I didn't start messing around with drugs. I urge people to stay away from drugs at all costs. Even though I'm sober and sane today, the thought of wanting to get high is still in my mind. That's how strong crack addiction is.

But, like the light-hearted reggae song says, life is what you make it. If you want to be a druggy, you'll be one. If you want to be successful in a career or start your own business, you can do that. You <u>can</u> achieve whatever you believe.

I thank God for delivering me from the sinister world of drugs. I appreciate things so much more now. It's feel great to have family that love you, support you, and back you up and it's even greater to have God at the center of your life. A God who will never leave you nor forsake you. We're so thankful for how much our family did for us when we were in need that Kathy and I have taken since in many children over the years that were in need of help. In fact, we have two kids staying with us now that didn't have anywhere to go. We're giving them the love, support, and guidance that they need just like we were given during our addiction.

All that time and money spent on drugs could have bought an island in the Pacific. But instead of letting it be a waste, I decided to share my crazy story to let it serve as a wake-up call so that people would know -- they could never fall too far for God to help them. They can do what they really want to do, if they put their minds to it and stay away from the influence of drugs.

I'll never forget when my mother said, "I'm so proud of you." I'll also never forget when my father said, "I'm not your father anymore; I'm your friend." Every time I saw them, they were happy to see me healthy and prospering.

My father passed away this year. He left this earth proud of the man I became. I thank God for my father and I'm so grateful that he got to witness my success. His words of wisdom echo in my ears more and more every day. "Don't be a follower, be a leader." "When you get successful, look out for the next person so that they can find success." I hope I'm doing just that by telling my story.

So, whoever you are, when you're at you're lowest and you think there's no way out, just remember these memoirs of a crackhead. Because if I can make it, so can you. May God Bless you always.

-Russell

Little Russell

Drug dealer Russell

Becoming an Electrician

Locked up at the
MD Correctional Facility

Russell & his sisters

Russell & Kathy

Cracked out Russell

92422518R00143

Made in the USA
Columbia, SC
27 March 2018